Uncle Sam's Retirement Plan

How to Protect Yourself
from His Sucker Punch

Charles Bartman

Charles Bartman, David Bartman,
and Michael Canet, JD, LLM

Uncle Sam's Retirement Plan
How to Protect Yourself from His Sucker Punch

ISBN: 978-1-956220-09-4

Disclaimer

Expert Press

www.ExpertPress.net

Table of Contents

Chapter 6

Chapter 7

Chapter 8

Chapter 9

Glossary

Introduction

Tax planning matters.

How often have you started a project at home that you thought you could do yourself but soon realized you were in way over your head? Whether it's because you tried and didn't finish the effort or you made a beginner's mistake, most of us are familiar with knowing when a specialist is best suited for a particular job. Financial services are no exception. From stocks and investments to tax planning, as an individual, you should proceed with extreme caution in an area that relates to your financial future.

Whether you are in the early stages of building your nest egg or meeting personal financial goals, many individuals begin by attempting the "do-it-yourself" approach. As income and wealth increase, it frequently becomes apparent that hiring a professional may make sense. A financial advisor is one such professional; a certified public accountant (CPA) or a tax accountant is another.

As experts in our field, we have observed all kinds of mistakes that people make when preparing for retirement. *Failing to plan for taxes leading into (and through) retirement is one of the biggest mistakes we regularly see.*

It's surprising in an industry such as this that we see so few professionals addressing clients' needs head-on. Tax planning is greatly important to Americans of all income levels. The majority of clients coming into our firm assume their CPA is maximizing tax savings for them. It's true that most CPAs do a good job filing returns for their clients. They make sure all the 1099s and W-2s or K-1s are properly filed, and they tell their clients how much they need to send to the Internal Revenue Service (IRS). However, this strategy isn't tax planning at its most efficient. What these CPAs typically do not do, at least proactively, is give advice on major tax strategies. The result is failure to use tax strategies that can save literally hundreds of thousands of dollars in current and future taxes.

We found that most clients need a holistic approach to their retirement. Sometimes this complete snapshot of their financial life can help avoid costly errors and tax inefficiencies. From our perspective, all investment advice and retirement planning should go through a rigorous tax review to address these inefficiencies. Only through this kind of comprehensive approach can you successfully navigate your retirement into a world of tax-free income.

So, how does this actually work?

What is Proactive Tax Planning?

Let's say a builder was getting ready to sell his construction business. The gain on the sale was substantial: $4,125,000. He had done a great job preparing for retirement, and his nest egg was almost enough to meet his retirement income needs, and certainly, there were the proceeds from selling his practice—including the real estate that would put him over the top of his income needs and goals for retirement. This builder was very interested in not only leaving a legacy for his children but also contributing to several charitable organizations.

He sat down with his CPA, the same CPA whose firm had handled all of the builder's business books and tax returns for years. When the CPA ran numbers for the builder, he calculated the gains and explained to the builder that the tax bill would be about $1 million. That's right: The CPA told the builder to be prepared to pay almost $1 million in taxes. *A million dollars in taxes!*

As you might imagine, the builder balked at the figure.

When we were presented with the opportunity to run our own scenarios, we stepped up to the challenge.

Want to save a *million dollars* in taxes?

The builder sure did, and we wanted to help him. With a little work and a little creativity, we were able to eliminate almost $900,000 of the tax bill.

Chapter 1

Why Taxes Matter

At the end of the day, it doesn't matter how much you make; it's how much you keep.

That is a pretty powerful statement when you realize that failing to consider the impact of taxes on your income, both now and in the future, could result in losing 30, 40, or even 50 percent of your income.

If taxes have that much impact, why is it that so little time is actually spent on tax planning? There are a couple of factors that come into play. Notably, the tax codes change almost every year, and there are literally thousands of pages of codes, regulations, rulings, and IRS guidance on how to apply the code.

During the debates over the 2017 Tax Cuts and Jobs Act, it was widely reported that there were over 70,000 pages of tax code. While that number isn't quite true, it comes close when considering all the information a person needs to know in order to actually provide smart tax-planning advice.

The tax code has nearly tripled in length over the last thirty years. Americans deserve a simpler, fairer, and flatter code.

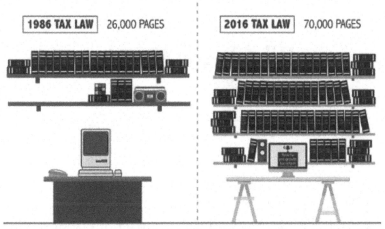

With a tax law that has nearly tripled in length in the last 30 years, it is no wonder that 9 out of 10 taxpayers now use either a professional tax preparer or computer software to file their taxes. **This blueprint delivers a simpler, fairer, and flatter tax code to help all Americans.**

█ = 1,000 PAGES

Given the limitation of time and expertise, regular Americans feel daunted about what they don't know and fearful of making errors. Statistically, nine out of ten individuals use professional or computer software for tax filing. Others, of course, prefer to work with in-dividuals who specialize in financial matters. However, even those who have (or hire) a financial advisor face obstacles. For example, most investment firms will not allow their advisors to provide tax guidance. Let that sink in. *The person you are relying on to help get you to and through retirement is not allowed to actually help you understand how your investments might be impacted by taxes.*

Let's take a look at a very simple example of why taxes matter. Let's assume that you and your spouse both work and have an annual combined income of $100,000. That puts you into the 22 percent tax bracket. Let's also assume that you take the standard deduction of $24,000. From your $100,000 mutual fund investment, you receive a 15 percent capital gains distribution. (Note: This doesn't necessarily mean you actually made money; consider 2008 and 2018, when the overall stock market was negative and many funds reported capitals gains in the 15 percent range.[1]) Let's also assume you have some savings and received $1,000 in earned interest—at least, here, you actually made money.

Here's the math:

W-2 Wages	$100,000
Capital Gains	15,000
Interest	1,000
Total Income	$116,000
Standard Deduction	(24,000)
Taxable Income	$92,000

---

1   https://www.morningstar.com/articles/890938/more-tax-pain-for-some-mutual-fund-shareholders-in-2018

The tax on $92,000, assuming 22 percent federal and 8 percent state taxes, is $20,305. This results in an effective tax rate of 17.5 percent.

Okay, so what is the point here? If on your $15,000 (generated from your investments) you are losing 17.5 percent each year, that tax cost reduces your future nest egg. Without this tax bite, an 8 percent return would grow to almost $151,000 over thirty years. Because of the tax bite, it only grows to just over $102,000. That is almost a 33 percent reduction in your nest egg—that's each year. That is huge. Would you accept a 33 percent pay cut? That is what you are doing when you don't pay attention to taxes.

Which brings us back to the point: How can a person provide investment advice without actually understanding the tax implications of that advice? How can you make your own investment decisions if you don't understand the tax implications?

Want further proof that taxes matter? Ask Warren Buffet. He is often quoted as saying that his tax rates are lower than his secretary's. Why is that? Warren has a crack team of tax attorneys at his disposal to take advantage of the tax laws.

Buffett does not usually release his tax returns, but he did so in 2010. On his return, he had an income of $39.8 million and paid taxes in the amount of $6.9 million. That's about a 17.3 percent effective tax rate. Warren understands that income subject to capital gains rates (currently between 0 and 20 percent) is much better than paying taxes at ordinary tax rates (currently up to 40.8 percent). To clarify: Buffett earned almost $40 million, and he paid the same tax rate as the couple in our example above, who made $116,000 in income. That is why tax planning matters.

Now that we can agree that tax planning matters, let's examine why taxes are poised to increase in the future.

Chapter 2

Debt Clocks and David Walker

First and foremost, think about the national debt. Is it going up or down?

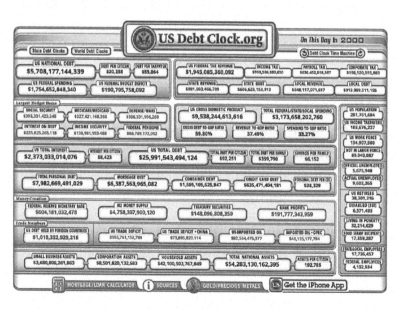

Since 2000, the national debt has gone from just under $6 trillion to over $29 trillion today. That is more than a 300 percent increase in debt.

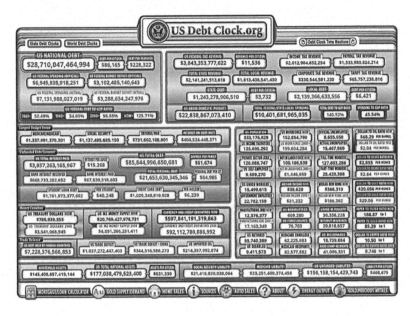

Source: USDebtClock.org_9-1-21

And look at the future obligations from the US debt clock.

In 2021, we will need to borrow over $1 trillion just to pay our bills. That means that almost 20 percent of our spending is deficit spending: We are borrowing money to pay our bills.[2]

How long can that be sustained without raising taxes at some point in the future? Let's take a look back for

---

2 https://www.wsj.com/articles/treasury-expects-to-borrow-1-3-trillion-over-second-half-of-fiscal-2021-11620068646

some guidance. In 2006, a CPA named David Walker went on a speaking tour, and he called it the "Fiscal Wake-Up Tour." During the tour across the country, Walker spoke to local and state governments, politicians, and every group who would take the time to listen to his dire warnings. In 2006, Walker was warning people about a "dirty little secret" everybody in Washington knows: We, as a country, are on a fiscal cliff, and if we don't do something to correct it, we will drive right over the edge. In 2006, Walker warned everybody about the nation's $8.5 trillion debt (now $29 trillion and counting, as of August 2021).

Walker spent almost two years telling anybody and everybody who would listen about how our nation was destined for a dire future if we weren't careful and making changes. He cautioned that now was the time to address these looming issues.

"Regardless of what politicians tell you, any additional accumulations of debt are . . . basically deferred tax increases."

Source: http://www.cnn.com/2009/POLITICS/04/15/walker.tax.debt/index.html?iref=24hour

Walker wanted to prove and share what he knew in his gut. With just simple math and instruction, Walker explained (to anyone who would listen) how there was not enough revenue coming into the Treasury to pay the bills. As a result, there was not enough money being collected by the US Treasury to pay the bills of today. Consequently, there was not enough money to pay future bills. This was a bad scene, one that would not correct itself without intervention or change.

Back in 2006, his cautions were important, but while he was talking about future obligations in the amount of $40–$50 trillion, he was actually off by a factor of almost two at the time, and this debt has only climbed over time. As of September 2021, we have over $85.5 trillion in future obligations, and the number continues to grow.

Think about it for a minute. George W. Bush added almost $7.5 trillion to the deficit in his eight years as president of the United States. Barack Obama added another $8.5 trillion in his eight years. Donald Trump added $6.5 trillion in his four years. Joe Biden, with the American Rescue, added $1.2 trillion to what was already projected to be a $2.3 trillion addition to the national debt.

It is clear that neither the Democrats nor Republicans are good stewards of our money. Do you think that any future president is actually going to spend less? The deficits will likely continue to grow, and the poor spending habits of our political leadership cannot address this problem. That means it becomes *your* problem. It will be *your* tax money.

Where will that money come from?

Again, Walker openly discussed his ideas and proved out scenarios using simple math. According to Walker, we would be required to raise taxes *and* cut benefits. Here is what he said:

> *If Social Security, Medicare, and Medicaid go unchanged, the rate for the lowest tax bracket would increase from 10 percent to 25 percent; the tax rate on incomes in the current 25 percent bracket would have to be increased to 63 percent, and the tax rate of the highest bracket would have to be raised from 35 percent to 88 percent.*[3]

3 https://www.cbo.gov/sites/default/files/110th-congress-2007-2008/reports/05-19- longtermbudget_letter-to-ryan.pdf

Demographics: It is All About the Baby Boomer

In his now-famous interview with CBS's *60 Minutes,* Walker described the problem with baby boomers and their drain on society.

Source: https://www.youtube.com/watch?v=U19_OkPRggE

Walker explained that the baby boomers, those born between 1946 and 1964, number about 76 million people. (Immigration offsets deaths, so 76 million is still the US Census number.[4]) Starting in 2008, boomers approaching retirement (age sixty-two or older) would become eligible for Social Security and be eligible for Medicare by 2011. That isn't the secret.

---

4 https://www.prb.org/justhowmanybabyboomersarethere/

The secret is that Social Security wasn't designed for 76 million people to collect their benefits for twenty or thirty years. Think back on your economics class from your youth. You may have learned about how Social Security was created and what it was designed to do. In August 1935, the life expectancy for the average American was about fifty-eight years of age for men and sixty-two years for women.[5] Even accounting for childhood deaths, only roughly 55 percent of those who made it to age twenty-one actually lived to collect Social Security.

What does this mean? A significant portion of those who paid into Social Security either never collected because of early death or had the common courtesy to die shortly after starting to collect their benefits.

On January 31, 1940, the first monthly retirement check was issued to Ida May Fuller of Ludlow, Vermont, in the amount of $22.54. Miss Fuller, a legal secretary, retired in November 1939.

Ida May Fuller worked for three years under the Social Security program. The accumulated taxes on her salary during those three years was a total of $24.75. Herinitial monthly check was $22.54.

5 https://www.ssa.gov/history/lifeexpect.html

> During her lifetime, she collected a total of $22,888.92 in Social Security benefits.

This means that, on average, most people collected Social Security for thirteen to fifteen years. However, this isn't a future-proof system. Many variables make this complicated. For example, people are now living much longer.[6] A ninety-year lifespan is not uncommon; 20 percent of men and 33 percent of women who reach age sixty-five will see their ninetieth birthday. While that's a lot of happy birthdays, that also means a bigger drain on Social Security and Medicare resources.[7]

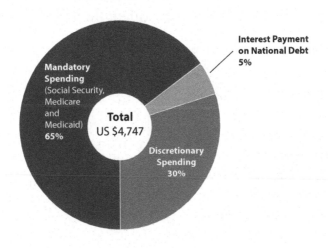

The Ballance Chart

Interest Payment on National Debt 5%

Mandatory Spending (Social Security, Medicare and Medicaid) 65%

Total US $4,747

Discretionary Spending 30%

Source: The White House

---

6 https://www.ssa.gov/OACT/NOTES/as120/LifeTables_Body.html

7 https://www.hamiltonproject.org/charts/probability_of_a_65_year_old_living_to_a_ given_age_by_sex_and_year

The US federal budget for FY 2021 is $6.011 trillion. That's $4.018 trillion in mandatory spending, which includes Social Security, Medicare, and Medicaid. That's $1.688 trillion in discretionary spending, which includes Defense, Education, and Energy. The interest payment on the national debt is $305 billion.[8]

We are currently spending almost 65 percent of our national revenue on mandatory items, with almost $2 trillion just on Social Security and Medicare. And that is with only being about halfway through the boomers wanting their benefits—we are set to hit "full" capacity of demand around 2026.

With that as the setting, let's look at the health of the Social Security Trust Fund and how much we have set aside to fund Medicare. According to the 2020 Social Security and Medicare Trust Fund Report, Social Security will be able to pay unreduced benefits until 2034, and Medicare has funding through 2026.[8]

This is an improvement—being fully funded until 2034. As recently as 2010, Social Security was actually posting grim statistics on their annual statements, warning people that by 2037 recipients will receive only about seventy-six cents on the dollar. That is almost a 25 percent decrease in income!

---

8 The Balance; "U.S. Federal Budget Breakdown: The Budge Components and Impact on the US Economy," by Kimberly Amadeo, updated July 15, 20201. https://www.thebalance.com/u-s-federal-budget-breakdown-3305789

For years, the Social Security Administration would send out an annual earnings statement to let you know about your reported earnings and the estimated amount you would receive in Social Security benefits in the future. They also let you know that Social Security was in deep financial trouble, going so far as to include the following paragraphs:

Now, however, the Social Security system is facing serious financial problems, and action is needed soon to make sure the system will be sound when today's younger workers are ready for retirement. [9]

In 2016 we will begin paying more in benefits than we collect in taxes. Without changes, by 2037, the Social Security Trust Fund will be exhausted, and there will be enough money to pay only about 76 cents for each dollar of scheduled benefits. [10]

We need to resolve these issues soon to make sure Social Security continues to provide a foundation of protection for future generations. [9]

The shortages faced by Social Security and Medicare go beyond people living longer and the baby boomers wanting their share. Remember that when Social Security first began in 1940, there were 159 workers supporting each recipient. Obviously, in 1940, not many people were actually receiving Social Security benefits. By 1960, there were 5.1 workers for each claimant, and by 2010,

---

9 Form SSA-7005-OL (01/15)

10 https://www.ssa.gov/policy/docs/ssb/v70n3/v70n3p111.html

there were only 2.9 workers supporting each claimant.[11] That number will continue to drop, and by 2035 it is estimated that the number will be closer to 2 to 1.[12]

Our unfunded liabilities, the money we owe for things like Social Security, Medicare, and the federal debt, exceed $122 trillion. You read that correctly: *$122 trillion.* Where is that money going to come from? Taxes.

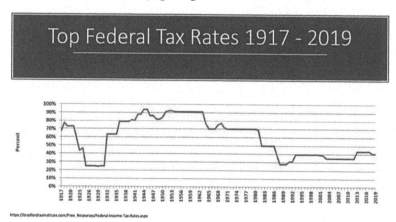

Top Federal Tax Rates 1917 - 2019

https://bradfordtaxinstitute.com/Free_Resources/Federal-Income-Tax-Rates.aspx

Where could tax rates go? No one knows for sure, but certainly, we have seen higher tax rates in our lifetimes. Let's reflect back on the history of a certain actor-president for a real-world example. During the 1940s, Ronald Reagan was an actor. As the story goes, he was paid about $100,000 for each film he made. The problem was, in the 1940s, the highest tax rate went all the way up to 94 percent on incomes above $200,000. This meant that Ronnie would make two movies a year and

11 https://www.ssa.gov/history/ratios.html

12 https://www.crfb.org/blogs/number-workers-social-security-retiree-declining

then pack up his things and go hang out on the ranch with his wife, Jane Wyman. Why? Because he didn't want to work for six cents out of every dollar.

By the time he became president in 1981, the top tax rates were 69.13 percent. That was almost a 25 percent reduction in tax rates. As we sit here in 2021, tax rates are still 37 percent. Could they go up? We know that they revert back to the tax rates that existed before the Tax Cuts and Jobs Act was passed. This means that people who are currently in the 12–22 percent tax bracket can expect to be in the 15–25 percent tax bracket. And that is if the tax rates only just revert back.

Consider this chart, showing the 2021 tax brackets:

Rate	For Unmarried Individuals	For Married Individuals Filing Joint Returns	For Heads of Households
10%	$0 to $9,950	$0 to $19,900	$0 to $14,200
12%	$9,951 to $40,525	$19,901 to $81,050	$14,201 to $54,200
22%	$40,526 to $86,375	$81,051 to $172,750	$54,201 to $86,350
24%	$86,376 to $164,925	$172,751 to $329,850	$86,351 to $164,900
32%	$164,926 to $209,425	$329,851 to $418,850	$164,901 to $209,400
35%	$209,426 to $523,600	$418,851 to $628,300	$209,401 to $523,600
37%	$523,601 or more	$628,301 or more	$523,601 or more

Taxes could even go as high as 100 percent. It doesn't seem possible or realistic, but Ed Slott, the CPA and retirement guru, tells a story that goes like this: It was around 1975 when John's father died, leaving John $1 million held inside his father's individual retirement account (IRA). It was the only asset his father owned. At the time, the estate tax rules allowed the first $60,000 to be passed tax free, and thereafter the tax rate was 58 percent. Because this was the only asset that John received, John had to take the money out of the IRA to pay the estate tax, which resulted in a tax rate of 70 percent on the withdrawal. Because John lived in California, the state imposed a tax of 11.5 percent.

Here's the math:

$1,000,000	Inherited from John's father
(60,000)	Estate tax exclusion
$940,000	Amount subject to estate tax
(545,200)	Estate tax that John had to pay from withdrawals from the IRA itself
(381,640)	Federal income tax on the $545,200 John was required to pay for estate tax
(62,698)	California income tax on the $545,200 John had to withdraw
$10,462	The balance left over for John

So, not quite 100 percent tax, but if you were told you just received $1,000,000 and after taxes all you had was $10,462, it might feel very much like they took 100 percent in taxes.

Can taxes go up? This 100 percent tax rate was available to each and every one of us in 1975. Could it be available again in 2022 or in the future? Time will tell. But given the fact that we as a nation spend more and more money each year, the national debt is growing by trillions each year, the future obligations of this country are in excess of $100 trillion dollars, and our political leaders seem unable or unwilling to address these spending habits, it would seem that David Walker is correct. These leaders will be forced to raise taxes *and* cut benefits.

Ed Slott and David Walker both agree: It does boil down to simple math. The best math results in being in the *zero*-income tax bracket. Why *zero*? Being in the *zero*-income tax bracket means that if the federal government raises taxes by 50 percent, your tax rate increase is still *zero*. If your state raises taxes by 25 percent, you are still in the *zero* percent tax bracket. *Zero* times any number is still *zero*.

Where to Start

You would think the starting point is to sit down with your CPA or your investment advisor and create a plan to become more tax efficient. That makes perfect sense, and it works in a perfect world. Unfortunately, for many people, their CPA is just somebody who puts numbers on a page, and their investment advisor just makes investment recommendations without truly understanding the tax implications.

Ken and Kathy came into the office with a very large investment portfolio. They had been working with the same investment firm for years. They had a CPA who had helped them with their very successful business and real estate holdings. They had recently retired and decided to simplify their lives. They sold their business and their real estate and settled into retirement.

When they first came into the office, we asked to see their tax returns, like any good planning firm should do. A tax return really does tell the financial story. We can see pretty much your whole life from your tax return. One of the things we noticed was that they were paying an exorbitant amount of capital gains taxes—to the tune of almost $83,000 a year—each year.

Filing Status
Check only one box.

☐ Single ☒ Married filing jointly ☐ Married filing separately (MFS) ☐ Head of household (HOH) ☐ Qualifying widow(er) (QW)

If you checked the MFS box, enter the name of your spouse. If you checked the HOH or QW box, enter the child's name if the qualifying person is a child but not your dependent ▶

Your first name and middle initial	Last name	Your social security number
KEN		123-45-6789
If joint return, spouse's first name and middle initial	Last name	Spouse's social security number
KATHY		234-56-7890

Home address (number and street). If you have a P.O. box, see instructions.			Apt. no.	Presidential Election Campaign
123 Your Street				Check here if you, or your spouse if filing jointly, want $3 to go to this fund. Checking a box below will not change your tax or refund.
City, town, or post office. If you have a foreign address, also complete spaces below.	State	ZIP code		
Foreign country name	Foreign province/state/county	Foreign postal code		☐ You ☐ Spouse

At any time during 2020, did you receive, sell, send, exchange, or otherwise acquire any financial interest in any virtual currency? ☐ Yes ☐ No

Standard Deduction

Someone can claim: ☐ You as a dependent ☐ Your spouse as a dependent

☐ Spouse itemizes on a separate return or you were a dual-status alien

Age/Blindness You: ☒ Were born before January 2, 1956 ☐ Are blind Spouse: ☒ Was born before January 2, 1956 ☐ Is blind

Dependents (see instructions):

(1) First name Last name	(2) Social security number	(3) Relationship to you	(4) ✓ if qualifies for (see instructions):	
			Child tax credit	Credit for other dependents
			☐	☐
			☐	☐
			☐	☐
			☐	☐

If more than four dependents, see instructions and check here ▶ ☐

	1	Wages, salaries, tips, etc. Attach Form(s) W-2		**1**	
Attach Sch. B if required.	**2a**	Tax-exempt interest	**2a**	b Taxable interest **2b**	1,450
	3a	Qualified dividends	**3a** 14,103	b Ordinary dividends **3b**	16,285
	4a	IRA distributions	**4a**	b Taxable amount **4b**	18,500
	5a	Pensions and annuities	**5a**	b Taxable amount **5b**	
Standard Deduction for—	**6a**	Social security benefits	**6a** 68,500	b Taxable amount **6b**	58,225
• Single or Married filing separately, $12,400	**7**	Capital gain or (loss). Attach Schedule D if required. If not required, check here . . . . ▶ ☐		**7**	595,765
	8	Other income from Schedule 1, line 9		**8**	
• Married filing jointly or Qualifying widow(er), $24,800	**9**	Add lines 1, 2b, 3b, 4b, 5b, 6b, 7, and 8. This is your total income . . . . ▶		**9**	690,225
	10	Adjustments to income:			
• Head of household, $18,650	**a**	From Schedule 1, line 22 . . . . **10a**			
	b	Charitable contributions if you take the standard deduction. See instructions **10b**			
• If you checked any box under Standard Deduction, see instructions.	**c**	Add lines 10a and 10b. These are your total adjustments to income . . . . ▶		**10c**	
	11	Subtract line 10c from line 9. This is your adjusted gross income . . . . ▶		**11**	690,225
	12	Standard deduction or itemized deductions (from Schedule A)		**12**	27,400
	13	Qualified business income deduction. Attach Form 8995 or Form 8995-A		**13**	0
	14	Add lines 12 and 13		**14**	27,400
	15	Taxable income. Subtract line 14 from line 11. If zero or less, enter -0-		**15**	662,825

> Line 7 includes rental income, sales of equities from their portfolio, and capital gain distributions from their mutual fund portfolio. The tax on those capital gains is almost $120,000, as shown on line 24. I know what you are thinking—"that isn't just capital gains tax, it includes taxes on the rest of their income." We'll address that "error in thinking" shortly.

16	Tax (see instructions). Check if any from Form(s): 1 ☐ 8814 2 ☐ 4972 3 ☐ _____ . . .	16	101,697
17	Amount from Schedule 2, line 3 .	17	
18	Add lines 16 and 17 .	18	101,697
19	Child tax credit or credit for other dependents .	19	
20	Amount from Schedule 3, line 7 .	20	
21	Add lines 19 and 20 .	21	
22	Subtract line 21 from line 18. If zero or less, enter -0- .	22	101,697
23	Other taxes, including self-employment tax, from Schedule 2, line 10 .	23	16,729
24	Add lines 22 and 23. This is your total tax . ▶	24	118,426
25	Federal income tax withheld from:		

It begged the question, *why*? When we reviewed the tax return, the first thing we wanted to know was, were they using the income generated by the capital gains, or was it being reinvested into the holdings? Their answer? Reinvestment. The couple's income needs were being met by their Social Security, rental income on a building they still owned, and the required minimum distributions from their IRAs.

They mentioned that their CPA explained that it was just part of making money. If you make money, you pay taxes. Their CPA's position was that it is the nature of investments. Their advisor explained that yes, they paid tax on the money, but that means they were making money. The fact is, they were doing pretty well with their investments. The problem was that they were losing so much to taxes, and each year they had to take away from their income rather than spend their income; they had to reserve a large portion of that income just to pay the tax on earnings they didn't use. Some taxes? *One hundred percent* of their monthly income from Social Security, rents, and RMDs had to be set aside just to cover the taxes on the investments. Imagine how that impacted their day-to-day living! They fell into the same trap that most people do. They relied on trusted advisors to help them with their money, and those advisors didn't truly understand taxes and tax planning.

Chapter 3

Tax Strategies That Work

Mutual funds are a very significant portion of many retirees' nest eggs. For years, the industry has pushed (think about all the ads you see on TV from mutual fund companies) for people to invest in the stock market via mutual funds. Almost all 401(k)s are stocked with mutual funds. Even the big wirehouses and brokerage firms push mutual funds on their clients. (The next time your advisor from a big box wirehouse recommends a mutual fund, ask them about soft dollar arrangements—but that is for another time and another book.) With so much effort put into directing us into mutual funds, is it any wonder that our CPAs and investment advisors don't focus on the tax implications of the very product being pushed?

For Ken and Kathy, the solution was quite simple. We suggested alternatives to mutual funds. We provided them with two approaches to their tax problems. First, they could transition their portfolio from their tax-heavy mutual funds into the more tax-efficient exchange-traded funds (ETFs).[13] By using ETFs, the capital gains are frequently reduced substantially just by the very nature of how they are structured. While this isn't meant to be a lesson in fund structure, it is important to understand that passive management typically results in less trading within the fund (less trading equates to fewer capital gains). In addition to reduced internal trading, an ETF trades like an individual stock. This means that you experience capital gains when *you* sell a position, not when *other* people redeem their interest in the mutual fund you also own.

A second option presented was the use of a low-cost, no-load (no commission) annuity. Annuities come with their own particular rules, but by using a no-load annuity, they could maintain their liquidity. And by using a low-cost annuity, we didn't run up against the *I-hate-annuities-and-you-should-too* issues; variable annuities are typically deemed to be high-expense ratio investment vehicles. What an annuity does do very effectively is eliminate the tax on any capital gains or earnings until such time as you actually use the money.

---

13 https://www.investopedia.com/articles/investing/090215/comparing-etfs-vs-mutual-funds-tax-efficiency.asp

An annuity acts like an IRA from the perspective that the investment returns, growth, interest, and capital gains are not taxed until they are actually withdrawn. At such time, any gains are taxed at ordinary tax rates, not capital gains rates.

We also explored how using life insurance as an investment vehicle could work. (We will address more about that approach later in this book.) Ken and Kathy ultimately decided that the best option for them was to transition into ETFs. By doing so, we were able to eliminate the majority of their capital gains exposure, reducing it down to about $16,000 a year and reducing their taxes substantially: They had over $80,000 in tax savings just by understanding the tax implications of their investments.

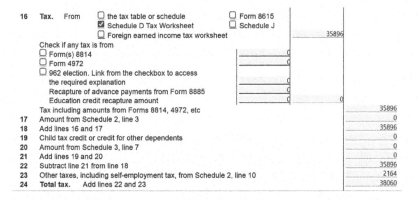

16	Tax. From ☐ the tax table or schedule ☑ Schedule D Tax Worksheet ☐ Foreign earned income tax worksheet	☐ Form 8615 ☐ Schedule J		35896
	Check if any tax is from ☐ Form(s) 8814 ☐ Form 4972 ☐ 962 election. Link from the checkbox to access the required explanation Recapture of advance payments from Form 8885 Education credit recapture amount		0 0 0 0	
	Tax including amounts from Forms 8814, 4972, etc			35896
17	Amount from Schedule 2, line 3			0
18	Add lines 16 and 17			35896
19	Child tax credit or credit for other dependents			0
20	Amount from Schedule 3, line 7			0
21	Add lines 19 and 20			0
22	Subtract line 21 from line 18			35896
23	Other taxes, including self-employment tax, from Schedule 2, line 10			2164
24	**Total tax.** Add lines 22 and 23			38060

Line 7 still includes $25,000 in rental income plus $187,000 in capital gains from their ETF portfolio (from their own personal selling, not from other people selling). The tax on those capital gains is only $28,000, with the rest of their income resulting in a total of $38,000 in taxes, as shown on line 24 *here*. Proper tax planning reduced their taxes by $80,000.

	1	Wages, salaries, tips, etc. Attach Form(s) W-2					1	
Attach Sch. B if required.	2a	Tax-exempt interest	2a		b Taxable interest		2b	1,450
	3a	Qualified dividends	3a	14,103	b Ordinary dividends		3b	16,285
	4a	IRA distributions	4a		b Taxable amount		4b	18,500
	5a	Pensions and annuities	5a		b Taxable amount		5b	
Standard Deduction for—	6a	Social security benefits	6a	68,500	b Taxable amount		6b	58,225
• Single or Married filing separately, $12,400	7	Capital gain or (loss). Attach Schedule D if required. If not required, check here ▶ ☐					7	212,500
	8	Other income from Schedule 1, line 9					8	
• Married filing jointly or Qualifying widow(er), $24,800	9	Add lines 1, 2b, 3b, 4b, 5b, 6b, 7, and 8. This is your total income ▶					9	306,960
	10	Adjustments to income:						
• Head of household, $18,650	a	From Schedule 1, line 22			10a			
	b	Charitable contributions if you take the standard deduction. See instructions			10b			
• If you checked any box under Standard Deduction, see instructions	c	Add lines 10a and 10b. These are your total adjustments to income ▶					10c	
	11	Subtract line 10c from line 9. This is your adjusted gross income ▶					11	306,960
	12	Standard deduction or itemized deductions (from Schedule A)					12	27,400
	13	Qualified business income deduction. Attach Form 8995 or Form 8995-A					13	0
	14	Add lines 12 and 13					14	27,400
	15	Taxable income. Subtract line 14 from line 11. If zero or less, enter -0-					15	279,560

The $80,000 they saved can now be used to further enjoy their retirement, which, for Ken and Kathy, meant making annual gifts to their three children. They were able to redirect $80,000 in what would otherwise have gone to the IRS, and instead gave $25,000 to each of their three kids. It all starts with understanding taxes.

Chapter 4

The Three Buckets: Taxable, Tax Deferred, and Tax Free

You have probably heard the phrase "buckets of money" if you have ever attended a financial workshop or read a book about retirement and money. There are basically three buckets of money:

① **Taxable**
② **Tax Deferred**
③ **Tax Free**

As a first step, set up your **three buckets** for money and label them accordingly.

A mathematically ideal amount of money should be in each bucket by the time you reach retirement. If you stopped reading here and had to guess, where do you think you'd want the bulk of your money?

How much is the ideal amount to be in each? That is where you need to sit down with a tax-planning professional who isn't necessarily a CPA or a financial advisor. This is somebody who truly understands tax planning and strategies that you can implement today and in the future, with the goal of creating a tax-free retirement for you and a tax-free legacy for your heirs. The key is to start planning for your tax-free retirement as soon as you possibly can.

Believe it or not, achieving a tax-free retirement is possible for everybody. It doesn't matter if you start the planning early in your working years or if you are already retired. With proper planning and implementing some of the strategies you will find in this book, you may be able to achieve the coveted *zero* percent tax bracket.

Bucket #1: the Taxable Bucket

Let's start with a simple understanding of what each bucket looks like. First, we have the taxable bucket. This is the bucket that contains assets on which you pay taxes each year: bank accounts, mutual fund accounts, stock accounts, and brokerage accounts.

At the end of every year, the bank issues you a 1099 for the amount of interest you have earned on your accounts. You then report that income on your tax return and pay the taxes accordingly.

Your mutual funds and your brokerage accounts may have a little twist attached to them: capital gains. This is that little stealth "income" you are forced to pay tax on regardless of whether you sold your mutual fund holdings and regardless of whether you actually made money on your investment. This is where the difference between working with a tax planner and working with a financial advisor comes into play.

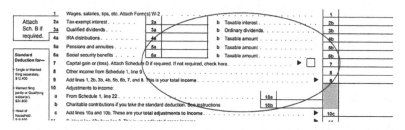

Your taxable bucket money is usually reported on lines 1-8 of your tax return.

The problem is that you are paying taxes on money you may not need or use. Going back to our simple math from earlier, does it make sense to give up 30 percent or more of your earnings to taxes, especially on money you don't use? To add insult to the tax injury, interest rates are so low at this point that it almost doesn't pay to save in interest-bearing accounts.

Bucket #2: the Tax-deferred Bucket

If you are receiving a W-2 from your employer, or even if you are self-employed, you need to sit down and do some math. Remember, it always boils down to simple math: today's tax bracket versus the tax bracket you will be in when you retire. Many of those who are saving toward retirement and their advisors subscribe to the belief that your retirement income will be in a lower tax bracket when you retire. The thought is that you will need less money during retirement. Why would you want to have less income when you retire?

James was an emergency room physician who had just retired after forty years of practice. Like many people, the good doctor was putting as much money away into his 401(k) as possible, getting advice every year from the 401(k) provider, and making good returns in his 401(k). He was earning a significant salary and was in the highest tax bracket for almost every year he worked, so reducing his salary via a 401(k) contribution made sense. In addition to his 401(k) contributions, at the recommendation of the 401(k) advisor/custodian, he was also making nondeductible contributions to his personal IRA and nondeductible contributions to his wife's IRA. Furthermore, he actually had a conversation with the 401(k) advisor; they assumed he would be in a lower tax bracket when he retired.

Why would you be in a lower tax bracket? Why would you want to be in a lower tax bracket? It seems that the only reason you might need less money during retirement than during your working years is if you were going to pay off a mortgage just as you enter into retirement. Even if that is your particular situation, it is certain that the "honey-do" list, the "get-around-to-it" list, and the "bucket" list are going to require additional income.

Many retirees no longer have the tax deductions they once had. Consider the fact that your mortgage balance is probably declining, which means less benefit from mortgage interest deductions.

Many retirees slow down their financial contributions to charity and start volunteering their time. Even those miscellaneous unreimbursed business expenses will be gone. If you or your advisor suggests that you will need less income during retirement, you may wish to revisit your math or find a better advisor.

For W-2 Employees: Tax Strategy #1

The common myth spread by CPAs and financial advisors is that it is better to defer your taxes until the future. This myth is based upon the idea that you will need less money in the future.

This myth has already been debunked: You will probably need as much, if not more, money during retirement and certainly during the first five to ten years as you are actively pursuing those bucket lists.

Here is the old way of thinking: Put as much into your 401(k) as your employer will allow, certainly up to any matching funds they provide. Hopefully, the goal is to maximize your 401(k) contributions each year. Here is the math:

$50,000	Taxable wages
(10,000)	401(k) contribution, which reduces your taxable wages
$40,000	Adjusted taxable wages reported on your tax return

The idea here is that your taxable wages are reduced each year, thereby saving you current tax dollars. The problem is that if you agree that tax rates are going to increase in the future, or even if you think tax rates may stay the same, then you are saving taxes on an apple seed today and being forced to pay taxes on all the apples in the future.

shutterstock.com • 271696475

The math suggests that it is better to pay taxes today on the seeds rather than on all the apples that come off the tree:

- Paying tax on the apples: $10,000 deferred today for thirty years (assuming 6 percent returns) is equal to $57,435. Take that lump sum out (assuming a 26 percent tax bracket), and you have a balance of $42,502.

- Paying tax on the seeds: The same $10,000 is deferred into a Roth 401(k) but with no tax savings, so the after-tax contribution value (to keep things fair) would be $7,400 (assuming the same 26 percent tax bracket). Defer that for thirty years, assume the same 6 percent rate of return, and you will have $42,502.

Wait, those are the same numbers. Isn't putting money into a Roth better? Wouldn't it save you taxes in the future? Well, the answer is yes, but there are many factors, and we'll address those a little later in this book. For now, if you choose to put money into a Roth 401(k) instead of the traditional 401(k) and taxes remain the same, then you are in the exact same position you would have otherwise been in—no harm, no foul.

However, if taxes go up, then paying tax on those seeds today makes a difference. If taxes go up as much as David Walker and the Congressional Budget Office have suggested they will, then your decision to pay taxes on the seeds has a profound impact.

- Paying tax on the apples: $10,000 deferred today for thirty years, assuming 6 percent returns, is equal to $57,435 after paying the 26 percent tax of $14,933, your balance is $42,502.

This is not a *significant* difference if taxes were to remain the same:

$57,435

(14,933)

$42,502

What happens if the tax rates go to the 63 percent bracket, as has been suggested? The difference is profound:

- Paying tax on the apples: $10,000 deferred today for thirty years, assuming 6 percent returns, is equal to $57,435. After paying the 63 percent tax of $36,184, your balance is $21,251.

This is certainly a *significant* difference, 50% more in taxes:

$57,435

(36,184)

$21,251

Paying tax on the seed could very well be better than paying tax on all those apples, especially if you think tax rates could go up even 1 percent, let alone double or more.

Bucket #3: the Tax-free Bucket

Consider using your company's Roth 401(k) instead of the traditional 401(k). Here, you pay tax on the seeds instead of the apples. There are rules that need to be followed, but this is the first step to tax-free retirement income.

There are a few rules to know when using a Roth 401(k). First, a Roth 401(k) is not a Roth IRA. They both have a few rules in common, but the Roth IRA has some additional rules, which will be addressed later. The most important thing to understand about making a contribution to your Roth 401(k) or Roth IRA is that you do not receive a tax deduction. Unlike a traditional 401(k) contribution, your contributions to your Roth 401(k) do not reduce your taxable income. That's the trade-off: *Pay the tax today to save the taxes later.*

You do have contribution limits: If you are under age fifty, for the tax year 2020, you are allowed to contribute up to $19,500. If you are over age fifty, there is a tax law provision called "catch up," which will allow you to contribute an additional $6,500. This means that for 2020, you can actually put up to $26,000 of your wages into a Roth 401(k).

There are also a few rules we need to follow when it comes time to making withdrawals from our Roths. First and foremost, the principal (that is, the amount you contributed) is never taxed. Second, you must wait at least five years before you can take the earnings out without them being subject to tax. And third, you must be over fifty-nine and a half years old to avoid the 10 percent early withdrawal penalty on those earnings.

The first rule can be easily overlooked. Your contribution is never taxed and is not subject to the 10 percent early withdrawal rule. In other words, you can contribute to a Roth and take the principal out whenever you want and not be taxed. That makes sense because you have already paid tax on that money. The second part of this rule says that your principal is not taxed even if withdrawn within five years and before age fifty-nine and a half, so you get to tell the IRS whether you have withdrawn earnings, principal, or both. You control your tax exposure.

Certainly, there are reasons that you would still want to put money into your 401(k) if the money is available. For James, the retired builder, there was most certainly a reason to have that 401(k) in place, but not for the reasons you probably think.

Remember, James had retired. When he retired, he and his 401(k) advisor, who was also the custodian of the 401(k), discussed rolling the 401(k) into his personal IRA. This makes perfect sense. Combining the accounts makes it easier to calculate RMDs when you turn seventy-two years old. An IRA has infinitely more investment options than a traditional 401(k). But for James and the advisor, it made sense. The advisor handled the 401(k) rollover, and it went perfectly:

- Direct rollover.

- No tax on the transfer.

- All handled correctly.

Perfect.

Except it wasn't.

Unfortunately for James, the advisor didn't understand the tax implications of combining the two accounts. Remember we said that James had been making nondeductible contributions for all those years? By combining the two accounts, James eliminated the ability to withdraw those contributions. By combining the two accounts, every time James took a dollar out, about five cents was a tax-free return of his principal (remember, a nondeductible contribution is never taxable).

And here was James's dilemma: He needed about $250,000 for a down payment on the retirement home he was having built in Florida. The 401(k) advisor told him he could take the money out of his IRA, but he would be losing 32 percent of that money to taxes. The recommendation from the advisor was to take out $370,000 so that he could have about $250,000 in his pocket. He even went to his CPA to calculate the taxes and the "five cents on every dollar he got back tax free."

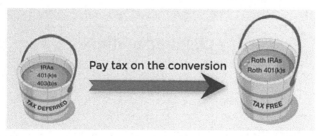

Our solution was to send him back to work. He got a part-time job at a local Boys Youth Club as a self-employed woodworking instructor. Over the course of eight months, he was paid almost $25,000, which was perfect and exactly what we wanted. We then opened a 401(k) for the retired builder. He contributed about $21,000 to the 401(k), which was the maximum he could add to his 401(k) because of FICA issues for self-employed people. The goal wasn't to get the $21,000 into a 401(k); the goal wasn't to put the builder back to work (his wife, Susan, was not very happy about him going back to work); the goal was to get a 401(k) open. You see, you can always roll an IRA into a 401(k), and we needed to get the after-tax dollars in that old IRA separated from the pre-tax dollars from the 401(k) rollover. And the beauty of it all is, while you can roll over pre-tax dollars, you can't roll over after-tax contributions.

We "cleaned" the account up. This meant that only after-tax dollars were left in his IRA. Yes, even the earnings on those after-tax dollars could be rolled over—just not the actual after-tax dollars. Once we cleaned up the account, the builder was able to withdraw the balance from the IRA and use those tax-free funds to build his house in Florida.

Tax planning matters.

Chapter 5

Finding a Tax Planner

Tax planning isn't a one-and-done activity. It is something you have to do each and every year. If you are currently working with a professional to prepare your taxes and that person isn't meeting with you several times a year to discuss tax-planning strategies, you are dealing with a tax preparer.

Quite frankly, you can teach a monkey to put numbers on a page. Today's tax software is very powerful and if you answer the questions they ask, you will get a return out of it. The problem here is twofold:

① **Understanding the reason behind the question**

② **Answering the question they are asking**

You can teach a monkey to put numbers on a page. That doesn't make the monkey more of a tax professional than someone with a CPA designation.

You need to use common sense. Tax software doesn't allow for common sense. It has to go through those 70,000 pages or so of tax rules, regulations, codes, and case law to determine what number needs to be put on the page. Ask a question. Get a number.

Working with a CPA does not guarantee that you will get better results or greater knowledge. Most CPAs are required to only take one tax course in order to qualify to sit for the exam (the requirement is based upon the underlying degree from a college or university; most accounting programs only require one class in taxation to receive a business or accounting degree). Even a CPA who has been preparing taxes for years may not offer tax-planning services to their clients.

CPAs do provide services like accounting and payroll. A good example of this type of client is the case of Paul and Jennifer. Paul owned a design company. It is actually a great business model. He works with homeowners who are remodeling their homes. His specialty is in the efficient use of space. It was interesting to see how much space in our homes isn't used effectively. He was really big on "floating shelves."

This small business provided Paul and his wife with a comfortable living, but it took a lot of work to keep track of mileage, inventory, sales, accounts receivable, and all the other aspects of owning a small business. Paul actually had a CPA firm doing his books for him and preparing his Schedule C each and every year. They told him how much to send in for estimated taxes. They told him how much profit he had. They even told him how much to put into his IRA every year. They were a good CPA firm. They didn't actually provide planning services, but they did make sure their numbers were in the right spot. Paul thought he had found a good tax professional.

Ask the Right Questions

If you want to work with a tax professional or an investment professional who does tax planning, you have to specifically ask if they provide *planning* services or just *preparation* services.

Ask the following questions:

1. How often should we meet to discuss taxes?

2. Do you need us to bring in our tax returns for your review?

3. Do you consider more than the current year in your planning?

4. How do you address retirement income?

5. Do you recommend various "money buckets"?

6. How long have you been providing planning services?

7. Will my Social Security be taxable?

8. Can you create a plan to get me to the *zero* percent tax bracket?

These are not simple questions and should not result in yes or no answers. They should respond with questions about where your money is currently held—taxable buckets, tax-free buckets, and tax-deferred buckets. They should ask about your income needs and discuss how long it will be before you retire. They should address a whole list of scenarios and be able to explain how they can attack the tax bite you may face in the future. Before they even give you advice, they should always ask to see your investments, and make sure they are also asking to see your tax returns. That should be part of the advice they are providing. *It doesn't matter how much you make; it is how much you keep.*

That is what we had in mind for Paul. Fortunately, he came to us before he finalized his tax return.

For Paul, the CPA was a person putting numbers on a page.

Paul's advisor was just facilitating the IRA contributions. *Paul had no tax planning.*

The CPA took Paul's QuickBooks reports, extracted the numbers from the P&L, and put them into the return. The CPA told Paul to make an IRA contribution for himself and his wife. The CPA told Paul that he would be writing a big check this year, a very large check. Paul was shocked. He was confused. His income wasn't that much larger than normal. In fact, when he came to see us, the first thing we did was fix this horrible tax issue.

Here was the problem. While Paul made a comfortable living with his interior design company, the cost of health insurance for a small businessman, like for many of us, was skyrocketing. He qualified for assistance under the Affordable Care Act. The ACA actually provided him with an up-front stipend to help pay the monthly premium. The ACA also had rules that needed to be followed. One of these rules was strict adherence to income. If a participant went one dollar over the threshold, they were forced to pay back their entire subsidy. All of it. Plus, there could be penalties. Paul was over the threshold and was in tax trouble. The CPA's solution was to pay the tax bill.

In Paul's case, we recommended opening a 401(k). By using a 401(k), he was able to put more money into the retirement account than he would put into a traditional IRA. In fact, we were going to use the same $12,000 he was going to contribute to his and his wife's IRAs, so that total went into the 401(k) instead. That didn't really make a difference as far as the ACA and tax bill went—after all, $12,000 out of the left pocket or out of the right pocket is still $12,000 out of the pocket. The CPA was quick to point this out when we suggested to them that Paul use a 401(k) instead of an IRA. Understanding how taxes work and tax planning was the difference between us and the CPA.

You see, 401(k) rules allow for the company— the company he owned—to share their profits (i.e., his profits) via a profit-sharing contribution to his 401(k). That is correct. In addition to "his" contributions to the 401(k), which reduces his personal income, the company can also make a contribution, which is called a profit-sharing match. This contribution also reduces Paul's total taxable income, but more importantly, it reduces his business income. Because of the nature of the ACA, reducing Paul's income by making IRA contributions wasn't enough. We needed to reduce the income of the business as well. This allowed him to qualify for the ACA, and therefore, he didn't have to repay the subsidy the CPA had him paying. The tax savings were just under $17,500.

Tax Planning Matters

Sitting down with your investment advisor probably isn't the solution either. If you have ever looked closely at your statements from your broker, they usually have a little disclaimer along the lines of:

- For tax advice, please consult with a qualified tax advisor, CPA, or financial planner. —Charles Schwab

OR

- Wells Fargo Advisors is a trade name used by Wells Fargo Clearing Services, LLC, a registered broker-dealer and non-bank affiliate of Wells Fargo & Company. We are not a legal or tax advisor.

OR

- Merrill Lynch would like you to note the following item(s) which may affect your tax return. Please discuss these matters with your Tax Advisor prior to completing your return.

And the list goes on.

Most investment professionals are not trained in and do not understand the complexities of tax planning. They may know simple rules such as those governing required minimum distributions (even then, there are disclaimers about talking to a tax professional), the difference between capital gains and ordinary income, and that Social Security may, in fact, be taxable. They are not tax planners, and most often, they make it clear that you need to talk to a tax professional. And therein lies the problem.

For many of those contemplating or entering into retirement, this is their first true encounter with a financial planning professional. Most advisors will gather some information about you and your situation: age, retirement date, assets, Social Security income, pension income, and a few other details like risk tolerance and the names of your heirs. They then compile a plan, based upon your risk tolerance, on how much money they think you can take from the portfolio they recommend to you. They may even take into account the fact that you will pay taxes, but more often than not, they are not making suggestions on how to allocate your investments based upon taxes. They want returns and growth; you want to know how much you actually get to keep.

Amy was this typical soon-to-be retiree. She was recently widowed and was going to receive a portion of her late husband's pension. It was a reasonable amount, and every penny counts when you are going from having a paycheck every two weeks to being unemployed for the next thirty years! She was going to collect Social Security. She had a 401(k) of her own and also had a very large equity position in a very specific stock. In fact, it was a stock that had been handed down through her family over several generations.

It was quite a story to hear about the changes and iterations of the ownership over the decades: Her great-grandfather started working in 1907 for a little automobile company called the Oakland Motor Car Company. For a short while, he worked the line. He then figured out that it was better to be a vendor and supply paint and painting equipment to the car company. Amy's great-grandfather started a private company, and each successive generation got into the family business. They supplied paint and supplies to everything from the Oaklands to the Pontiacs, and even to the Cadillacs. While Amy went into the automobile industry, she didn't join the family business. By the time she graduated from college, the company had grown quite large and was actually traded on the exchange. Amy loves sharing the story because it is part of her history.

When Amy sat down with her advisor, he explained to her that she would need to sell her investment of stock in order to diversify (sounds reasonable), and once she sold and diversified, she would be able to use those proceeds to help create the income she needed during retirement. The advisor had a simple approach to her income need. Amy had income from pensions and Social Security, along with a required minimum distribution (RMD) calculation that would produce a certain number of dollars from her IRA. So to secure her income, the advisor wanted to invest a large portion of the proceeds from the sale of the stock into an annuity.

As Amy understood, the annuity would guarantee her an income stream, regardless of the market conditions, for the remainder of her life. Again, all of this sounds reasonable (you can argue the pros and cons of using annuities, but that is another story).

When Amy presented her plan to the CPA she had been working with for decades, they asked about the basis of the stock to calculate the taxes Amy would have to send to the IRS. Amy explained the history of inheriting the stock from her grandfather almost forty years ago. She explained the buying, selling, and mergers of the company itself over the years, and based upon those facts, the CPA calculated that Amy would have a gain of about $773,498 and would be paying about $116,000 in taxes.

Amy was a bit surprised, but she understood there would be a tax bill associated with the sale of the stock, per the advice of her financial advisor. She understood the need to create income and the need for diversification. It all sounded reasonable.

Then her son found out what she was doing and asked her to sit down with us and allow us to review the plan the advisor had created. Immediately, our concern focused on two issues: the basis of the stock being sold and the investment recommendations being made.

Amy explained to us that the CPA had been doing her taxes since she inherited the stocks from her grandfather. In fact, she had the original transfer paperwork for the inheritance, and it actually had a price per share on the document. We had a starting point. We then asked her whether she had been receiving dividends and distributions over the years, and the answer was yes. As a matter of fact, the CPA had shown her every year how much she was earning on the inheritance. This meant that we had a record of each financial transaction that happened in the past.

You see, for Amy, each time she received a dividend on paper, the company actually kept the dividends for operating expenses. This meant that all those dividends actually added to her basis. By the time we were done reviewing and analyzing her taxes, we were able to reduce them to just an $87,000 gain. But the good news didn't end there.

We also did some tax planning for her based on the recommendations of her advisor. Amy had told her advisor that she wanted $140,000 a year to live on. It was a nice retirement. The advisor knew that she would receive about $36,000 in pensions and $43,000 in Social Security. That left him to find the balance of $62,000 per year. In order to do this, he recommended using an annuity. The annuity would produce the $62,000 per year she wanted if she put just over $900,000 into the contract. Coincidentally, that was about the balance left over after paying her tax bill, according to the return her CPA wanted to file.

Here is the problem we had (and there were several) from a tax perspective. The advisor was solving an income issue but ignoring the tax issue. By using her after-tax dollars and putting them into an annuity, he did create the income she wanted, but in doing so, the growth, interest, and earnings that came out of the annuity would all be taxed at ordinary tax rates. The tax bill wasn't pretty, *and* it resulted in her having less than the $140,000 she wanted. Remember, there was a tax bill due each year.

Your first name and middle initial AMY	Last name			Your social security number 123-45-6789
If joint return, spouse's first name and middle initial	Last name			Spouse's social security number

Home address (number and street). If you have a P.O. box, see instructions. 123 Your Street			Apt. no.	Presidential Election Campaign Check here if you, or your
City, town, or post office. If you have a foreign address, also complete spaces below.	State	ZIP code		spouse if filing jointly, want $3 to go to this fund. Checking a box below will not change
Foreign country name	Foreign province/state/county	Foreign postal code		your tax or refund. ☐ You ☐ Spouse

At any time during 2020, did you receive, sell, send, exchange, or otherwise acquire any financial interest in any virtual currency? ☐ Yes ☐ No

Standard Deduction — Someone can claim: ☐ You as a dependent ☐ Your spouse as a dependent
☐ Spouse itemizes on a separate return or you were a dual-status alien

Age/Blindness You: ☒ Were born before January 2, 1956 ☐ Are blind Spouse: ☐ Was born before January 2, 1956 ☐ Is blind

Dependents (see instructions):

(1) First name Last name	(2) Social security number	(3) Relationship to you	(4) ✓ if qualifies for (see instructions): Child tax credit	Credit for other dependents
			☐	☐
			☐	☐
			☐	☐
			☐	☐

1	Wages, salaries, tips, etc. Attach Form(s) W-2				1	
2a	Tax-exempt interest	2a	b Taxable interest		2b	
3a	Qualified dividends	3a	b Ordinary dividends		3b	
4a	IRA distributions	4a	b Taxable amount		4b	36,000
5a	Pensions and annuities	5a	b Taxable amount		5b	62,000
6a	Social security benefits	6a 43,000	b Taxable amount		6b	36,550
7	Capital gain or (loss). Attach Schedule D if required. If not required, check here ☐				7	
8	Other income from Schedule 1, line 9				8	
9	Add lines 1, 2b, 3b, 4b, 5b, 6b, 7, and 8. This is your total income				9	134,550
10	Adjustments to income:					
a	From Schedule 1, line 22		10a			
b	Charitable contributions if you take the standard deduction. See instructions		10b			
c	Add lines 10a and 10b. These are your total adjustments to income				10c	
11	Subtract line 10c from line 9. This is your adjusted gross income				11	134,550

Form 1040 (2020)   AMY   123-45-6789   Page **2**

16	Tax (see instructions). Check if any from Form(s): 1 ☐ 8814 2 ☐ 4972 3 ☐ ___				16	23,000
17	Amount from Schedule 2, line 3				17	
18	Add lines 16 and 17				18	23,000
19	Child tax credit or credit for other dependents				19	
20	Amount from Schedule 3, line 7				20	
21	Add lines 19 and 20				21	
22	Subtract line 21 from line 18. If zero or less, enter -0-				22	23,000
23	Other taxes, including self-employment tax, from Schedule 2, line 10				23	
24	Add lines 22 and 23. This is your total tax				24	23,000

After reviewing Amy's taxes and investment options with her, we made a few adjustments. We wanted to preserve the capital gains nature of her investments.

What the CPA failed to explain, what the investment advisor didn't understand, and what Warren Buffet knows all too well is that when you can't have tax-free income, you can have qualified dividends and capital gains. Why? Because if you handle dividends and capital gains correctly, your tax rate is *zero*, which means that you pay no tax on your capital gains or your qualified dividends.

Form **1040**	Department of the Treasury—Internal Revenue Service (99) **U.S. Individual Income Tax Return**	**2020**	OMB No. 1545-0074	IRS Use Only—Do not write or staple in this space.

Filing Status
Check only one box.

[X] Single [ ] Married filing jointly [ ] Married filing separately (MFS) [ ] Head of household (HOH) [ ] Qualifying widow(er) (QW)

If you checked the MFS box, enter the name of your spouse. If you checked the HOH or QW box, enter the child's name if the qualifying person is a child but not your dependent ▶

Your first name and middle initial	Last name	Your social security number
AMY		123-45-6789
If joint return, spouse's first name and middle initial	Last name	Spouse's social security number

Home address (number and street). If you have a P.O. box, see instructions. Apt. no.
123 Your Street

City, town, or post office. If you have a foreign address, also complete spaces below.	State	ZIP code

Foreign country name	Foreign province/state/county	Foreign postal code

Presidential Election Campaign
Check here if you, or your spouse if filing jointly, want $3 to go to this fund. Checking a box below will not change your tax or refund. [ ] You [ ] Spouse

At any time during 2020, did you receive, sell, send, exchange, or otherwise acquire any financial interest in any virtual currency? [ ] Yes [ ] No

Standard Deduction
Someone can claim: [ ] You as a dependent [ ] Your spouse as a dependent
[ ] Spouse itemizes on a separate return or you were a dual-status alien

Age/Blindness You: [X] Were born before January 2, 1956 [ ] Are blind Spouse: [ ] Was born before January 2, 1956 [ ] Is blind

Dependents (see instructions):
If more than four dependents, see instructions and check here ▶ [ ]

(1) First name Last name	(2) Social security number	(3) Relationship to you	(4) ✓ if qualifies for (see instructions): Child tax credit / Credit for other dependents

Attach Sch. B if required.	1	Wages, salaries, tips, etc. Attach Form(s) W-2		1	
	2a	Tax-exempt interest	2a	b Taxable interest 2b	
	3a	Qualified dividends	3a 55,000	b Ordinary dividends. 3b	500
Standard Deduction for—	4a	IRA distributions	4a 42,000	b Taxable amount 4b	32,000
• Single or Married filing separately, $12,400	5a	Pensions and annuities	5a	b Taxable amount 5b	
• Married filing jointly or Qualifying widow(er), $24,800	6a	Social security benefits . . .	6a 43,000	b Taxable amount 6b	21,500
	7	Capital gain or (loss). Attach Schedule D if required. If not required, check here . . . . ▶ [ ]		7	
• Head of household, $18,650	8	Other income from Schedule 1, line 9		8	
	9	Add lines 1, 2b, 3b, 4b, 5b, 6b, 7, and 8. This is your total income . . . . ▶		9	54,000
	10	Adjustments to income:			
	a	From Schedule 1, line 22	10a		
	b	Charitable contributions if you take the standard deduction. See instructions	10b		
	c	Add lines 10a and 10b. These are your total adjustments to income . . . . ▶		10c	
	11	Subtract line 10c from line 9. This is your adjusted gross income . . . . ▶		11	54,000

> By preserving the capital gains aspect of Susan's income, she now enjoys just over $140,000 a year of tax-free income.

Notice that line 11 shows $54,000 in income. That is the income that is subject to tax. Look at boxes 3a, 4a, and 6a. That is real income, and it equals the $140,000 Amy wants for retirement.

Amy's income has increased by almost 20 percent, and she now pays *zero* taxes.

household, $18,650	11	Subtract line 10c from line 9. This is your adjusted gross income . . . . ▶	11	54,000
• If you checked any box under Standard Deduction, see instructions	12	Standard deduction or itemized deductions (from Schedule A)	12	14,050
	13	Qualified business income deduction. Attach Form 8995 or Form 8995-A	13	0
	14	Add lines 12 and 13	14	14,050
	15	Taxable income. Subtract line 14 from line 11. If zero or less, enter -0-	15	39,950

For Disclosure, Privacy Act, and Paperwork Reduction Act Notice, see separate instructions.   Form **1040** (2020)

BCA

Form 1040 (2020)   AMY   123-45-6789   Page **2**

16	Tax (see instructions). Check if any from Form(s): 1 ☐ 8814 2 ☐ 4972 3 ☐ _____ . . .	16	
17	Amount from Schedule 2, line 3	17	
18	Add lines 16 and 17	18	
19	Child tax credit or credit for other dependents	19	
20	Amount from Schedule 3, line 7	20	
21	Add lines 19 and 20	21	
22	Subtract line 21 from line 18. If zero or less, enter -0-	22	
23	Other taxes, including self-employment tax, from Schedule 2, line 10	23	
24	Add lines 22 and 23. This is your total tax . . . . ▶	24	

Tax planning matters.

Understanding Tax Free

If you don't know anything else at this point, which bucket would you choose to hold the majority of your money? At the end of the day, there is a mathematically correct amount of money to have in each of the three buckets.

What exactly constitutes tax free? Three basic vehicles provide for tax-free income. Before we get there, we need to take a step back and examine Social Security again.

It is often thought that Roosevelt said, "Social Security would never be taxed." In fact, there were several administrative rulings from the Treasury Department in the '30s and '40s that exempted Social Security payments from tax. This was true all the way up to 1983. In 1981, President Reagan and Congress passed the Economic Recovery Tax Act and the ensuing tax law changes, including the Equity and Fiscal Responsibility Act of 1982 and the 1983 Amendments to the Social Security Act, resulting in up to 50 percent of Social Security being exposed to taxes. In 1993, as part of the Omnibus Budget Reconciliation Act, up to 85 percent of Social Security was now subject to tax exposure.[14]

Here is how this works.

First, add up all your provisional income. Your provisional income is basically all your income that will appear on your tax return except Social Security. The rule requires you to include all the income that will show up on the return, but it does not allow you to take any of the adjustments that would reduce your income. For example, you do not reduce your provisional income by your IRA contributions, your self-employ-

14 https://www.ssa.gov/history/taxationofbenefits.html

ment health care deductions, or any of those items that are included in calculating your Modified Adjusted Gross Income.

7	Wages, salaries, tips, etc. Attach Form(s) W-2	**7**	
8a	Taxable interest. Attach Schedule B if required	**8a**	
b	Tax-exempt interest. **Do not** include on line 8a . . . `8b`		
9a	Ordinary dividends. Attach Schedule B if required	**9a**	
b	Qualified dividends . . . . `9b`		
10	Taxable refunds, credits, or offsets of state and local income taxes	**10**	
11	Alimony received	**11**	
12	Business income or (loss). Attach Schedule C or C-EZ	**12**	
13	Capital gain or (loss). Attach Schedule D if required. If not required, check here ▶ ☐	**13**	
14	Other gains or (losses). Attach Form 4797	**14**	
15a	IRA distributions . `15a`	b Taxable amount . . .	**15b**	
16a	Pensions and annuities `16a`	b Taxable amount . . .	**16b**	
17	Rental real estate, royalties, partnerships, S corporations, trusts, etc. Attach Schedule E	**17**	
18	Farm income or (loss). Attach Schedule F	**18**	
19	Unemployment compensation	**19**	
20a	Social security benefits `20a`	b Taxable amount . . .	**20b**	
21	Other income. List type and amount	**21**	
22	Combine the amounts in the far right column for lines 7 through 21. This is your **total income** ▶	**22**	
23	Educator expenses	**23**	
24	Certain business expenses of reservists, performing artists, and fee-basis government officials. Attach Form 2106 or 2106-EZ	**24**	
25	Health savings account deduction. Attach Form 8889 .	**25**	
26	Moving expenses. Attach Form 3903	**26**	
27	Deductible part of self-employment tax. Attach Schedule SE .	**27**	
28	Self-employed SEP, SIMPLE, and qualified plans . .	**28**	
29	Self-employed health insurance deduction	**29**	
30	Penalty on early withdrawal of savings	**30**	
31a	Alimony paid **b** Recipient's SSN ▶	**31a**	
32	IRA deduction	**32**	
33	Student loan interest deduction	**33**	
34	Tuition and fees. Attach Form 8917	**34**	
35	Domestic production activities deduction. Attach Form 8903	**35**	
36	Add lines 23 through 35		
37	Subtract line 36 from line 22. This is your **adjusted gross income** . . . . . ▶		

Provisional income does not allow you to reduce your income by adjustments.

Once you have calculated your provisional income (don't forget to include municipal-bond and other tax-free interest into the calculation), add that to one-half of your Social Security.

7	Wages, salaries, tips, etc. Attach Form(s) W-2			7	
8a	**Taxable interest.** Attach Schedule B if required			8a	1000
b	Tax-exempt interest. **Do not include on line 8a**	8b	500		
9a	Ordinary dividends. Attach Schedule B if required			9a	5000
b	Qualified dividends	9b			
10	Taxable refunds, credits, or offsets of state and local income taxes			10	
11	Alimony received			11	
12	Business income or (loss). Attach Schedule C or C-EZ			12	
13	Capital gain or (loss). Attach Schedule D if required. If not required, check here ▶ ☐			13	10000
14	Other gains or (losses). Attach Form 4797			14	
15a	IRA distributions	15a	b Taxable amount	15b	10000
16a	Pensions and annuities	16a	b Taxable amount	16b	10000
17	Rental real estate, royalties, partnerships, S corporations, trusts, etc. Attach Schedule E			17	
18	Farm income or (loss). Attach Schedule F			18	
19	Unemployment compensation			19	
20a	Social security benefits	20a	25000	b Taxable amount	20b	21250
21	Other income. List type and amount			21	
22	Combine the amounts in the far right column for lines 7 through 21. This is your **total income** ▶			22	57250

85 percent of Social Security is taxable.

The provisional income is calculated as follows:

Taxable Interest	$1,000.00
Tax-Free Interest	500.00
Dividends	5,000.00
Capital Gains	10,000.00
IRA Distribution	10,000.00
Pension	10,000.00
Subtotal	$36,500.00
½ of SS of $25,000.00	12,500.00
Total:	$49,000.00

Married Filing Jointly

Provisional Income	% of Social Security Subject to Tax
Under $32,000	0%
$32,000 to $44,000	50%
Over $44,000	85%

Single Filers

Provisional Income	% of Social Security Subject to Tax
Under $25,000	0%
$25,000 to $34,000	50%
Over $34,000	85%

So what counts as tax free? Any item that does not cause Social Security to be subject to taxation. For our conversation, those three categories are Roth 401(k)s, Roth IRAs, and properly designed cash-value life insurance. We have already explained how the Roth 401(k) works. Let's examine the other two sources of tax-free income.

The Roth IRA shares the same features as a Roth 401(k). They both have a five-year requirement to avoid tax on the growth. They both have until age fifty-nine and a half to avoid penalties on their withdrawals of the growth. Where the 401(k) and the IRA differ dramatically is in the ability to contribute to them. The Roth 401(k) has no income limitations on a person's ability to contribute to it.

Conversely, the Roth IRA does have restrictions on the ability to contribute. First, you must have income to contribute. For our purposes, this means either you have wages reported on a W-2, or you are self-employed, and your profit is subject to FICA (Social Security and Medicare) taxes. If you have income, you are eligible to contribute to your Roth IRA. In 2021, people under age fifty can contribute up to $6,000 (your contribution is subject to your earnings; you cannot contribute more than you make). People over age fifty can contribute a "catch up" of an additional $1,000. So, for 2021, you can contribute up to $7,000 of your wages into a Roth IRA.

The next rule that needs to be observed concerns your total income. While there are no earning limitations on the Roth 401(k), there are limitations when it comes to contributing to a Roth IRA. For single filers, the 2021 rules begin to limit your allowable contributions when your income reaches $125,000, and by the time your income exceeds $140,000, your ability to contribute is completely phased out. For married filers, the phase-out begins at $198,000 and ends at $208,000. Basically, if you make too much money, you can't take advantage of a Roth IRA.

However, for those constrained by the income limitations—lucky you!—there are strategies to work around the rules. This is where tax planning comes into play again. What is the strategy? It is called a "back-door Roth." The idea is similar in nature to what we did for James when he rolled his 401(k) into his nondeductible IRA.

Here is what you do: Make a nondeductible IRA contribution. You can then immediately convert the nondeductible IRA into a Roth. For conversions, there are no income rules. This means that anybody, regardless of income, can convert from an IRA or 401(k) (or another company-sponsored retirement plan) into a Roth IRA, thereby turning what would otherwise be a taxable account into a lifetime of tax-free income for you and your heirs.

Roth Conversions

Pay tax today at lower tax rates to have tax-free money later when tax rates are higher.

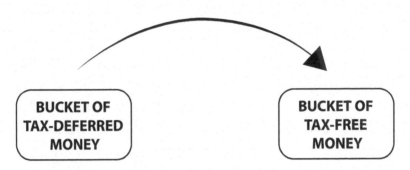

The idea behind a Roth conversion is that we want to move our money out of the tax-deferred bucket and pay taxes at today's rates so that when we use the money down the road, the money is tax free. This goes back to the idea of paying tax on the seeds instead of the apple. Before you jump aboard the conversion bandwagon, it does take a little math and strategy to determine whether this type of conversion makes sense for you.

Remember Ken and Kathy? Their capital gains problem was just the tip of the iceberg. When we were reviewing their investments and retirement plan, we discovered another inconsistency between good planning, their advisor, and their CPA. Their advisor actually told them to convert some of their IRA money into a Roth. Sounds like good advice, right? They took that advice to their CPA, and during the meeting, without having done any actual review or analysis, the CPA said that converting wasn't a good idea. Ken and Kathy had a real problem. One advisor was telling them to convert; the other advisor was saying <u>not</u> to convert. This advisor was telling them that they would save money on taxes later. The CPA was saying that the tax consequences today were too drastic.

If you remember, Ken and Kathy were really big on helping their kids out. They also had all the income they needed, and because we suggested the couple restructure their investments, there was more than enough cash flow to meet their needs without actually using the RMDs they were forced to take out each year.

Comparison of Alternatives

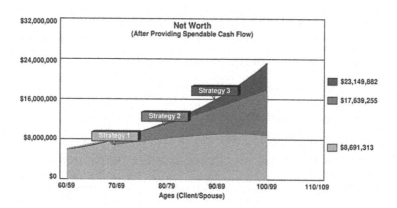

What Ken and Kathy wanted to know was whether it made sense to convert from their traditional IRA to the Roth. The answer for them was yes. It made sense, but first they wanted to understand the rules of how and why. Those rules, while they seem simple and straightforward enough, are actually quite complicated.

The first thing to consider is what tax rate you are in today and what tax rate you will be in when you retire. If you are already retired, this turns out to be an easy exercise. The tricky part is figuring out what your tax rate will be when you retire. It is a bit like hitting a moving target. Do you just use the existing tax rates and assume what your income needs will be? Do you assume that tax rates will be greater in the future? If so, then what rate will that be?

We know that many tax cuts in the past have contained "sunset" provisions; that is, the tax cuts are temporary and "sunset," or go away and revert back to prior tax rates. President George W. Bush signed the Economic Growth and Tax Relief Reconciliation Act of 2001, providing various levels of tax relief across the board. These provisions contained a sunset provision, so they were due to expire in 2010.

President Obama and Congress extended those tax breaks in 2010 as part of their budget deals. In 2012, some of those tax breaks were made permanent.

As with the Reagan tax cuts in 1981's Economic Recovery Tax Act, none of them delivered the promised growth that would, in turn, generate enough new tax revenue to cover the budget deficit. Tax cuts such as these three give credence to David Walker's concern about the growing deficit.

In 2017, President Trump signed into law the Tax Cuts and Jobs Act, significantly lowering corporate taxes as well as lowering taxes for individuals. These tax cuts also contain sunset provisions.

For example, in 2021, the 12 percent tax bracket for married (filing jointly) taxpayers covers between $19,901 and $81,050 of taxable income. In 2026, that same couple, with income between $18,650 and $75,900, will be taxed at 15 percent, and income between $75,901 and $153,100 will be taxed in the 25 percent tax bracket.

You will want to explore where you think you will fall, tax bracket-wise, today as well as in the future.

Obviously, you will need to take into account your sources of income: pensions, Social Security, investments, real estate, retirement accounts, and wherever else your income might flow. Once you know your income sources, you then have to run tax calculations on those flows.

Once you have calculated those taxes, you then have to consider your current income and add in the amount you might want to convert from your retirement accounts to your Roth account. Remember, you have to pay tax when you move your assets from a traditional IRA or 401(k) into the Roth IRA (this is called a conversion). What tax bracket will you be in if you choose to convert? There is a tax bill due. You are paying the tax today so that in theory, you will save in taxes later.

In addition to determining what the additional tax will be, you also have to determine from where the tax bill will be paid. Paying for the tax out of the conversion itself could be an option. But remember, if you were to use the actual IRA itself to pay the tax bill, it counts as a withdrawal and therefore could be subject to a 10 percent penalty if you are under age fifty-nine and a half. And the use of the IRA money itself could mean it takes longer for the Roth to actually "catch up" for the tax money withdrawn. You might be better off paying the tax from dollars that are already taxed: Use the taxable bucket!

Net Worth*			Wealth to Heirs		
Strategy 1	Strategy 2	Strategy 3	Strategy 1	Strategy 2	Strategy 3
47.14%	23.57%	Tax Efficient	47.14%	23.57%	Tax Efficient
6,001,533	6,001,533	5,981,920	5,616,080	5,616,080	7,845,257
6,206,025	6,206,025	6,092,442	5,759,345	5,759,345	7,915,158
6,381,616	6,381,616	6,247,906	5,926,667	5,926,667	8,011,448
6,580,228	6,580,228	6,428,849	6,114,244	6,114,244	8,129,419
6,784,329	6,784,329	6,618,050	6,307,188	6,307,188	8,251,633
6,994,032	6,994,032	6,829,124	6,505,624	6,505,624	8,378,307
7,209,452	7,209,452	7,049,385	6,709,675	6,709,675	8,509,680
7,430,702	7,430,702	7,279,343	6,919,468	6,919,468	8,646,000
7,657,898	7,657,898	7,519,546	7,135,130	7,135,130	8,787,535
6,707,174	7,891,150	7,770,562	7,266,608	7,356,785	8,934,568
6,834,439	8,130,571	8,046,896	7,397,390	7,584,561	9,158,314
6,961,475	8,375,902	8,333,064	7,527,201	7,821,455	9,389,739
7,088,059	8,627,166	8,629,292	7,655,746	8,064,918	9,629,085
7,213,944	8,884,370	8,935,813	7,782,702	8,315,041	9,838,705
7,338,869	9,147,506	9,252,846	7,907,726	8,571,916	10,024,173
7,462,544	9,416,557	9,580,610	8,030,444	8,835,623	10,216,748
7,584,663	9,691,477	9,919,290	8,150,455	9,106,229	10,416,709
7,704,892	9,972,223	10,269,078	8,267,327	9,383,695	10,624,167
7,822,878	10,258,720	10,630,154	8,380,601	9,595,254	10,839,585
7,938,230	10,550,882	11,002,798	8,489,773	9,809,093	11,063,058
8,050,539	10,848,607	11,387,275	8,594,317	10,028,978	11,294,873
8,159,361	11,151,771	11,783,807	8,693,657	10,254,981	11,535,326
8,264,218	11,460,222	12,192,842	8,787,184	10,487,158	11,784,713
8,364,598	11,773,789	12,615,130	8,874,239	10,725,549	12,043,341
8,459,957	12,092,269	13,051,493	8,954,124	10,970,179	12,311,520
8,549,703	12,415,459	13,503,030	9,026,083	11,220,729	12,589,212
8,633,210	12,743,135	13,971,591	9,089,319	11,477,061	12,850,281
8,709,806	13,075,049	14,458,807	9,142,971	11,739,079	13,082,851
8,778,772	13,410,927	14,967,649	9,186,126	12,006,646	13,322,482
8,839,339	13,750,466	15,502,072	9,217,803	12,279,580	13,606,483
8,890,688	14,093,381	16,062,248	9,236,962	12,557,177	13,959,036
8,931,940	14,439,371	16,644,823	9,242,488	12,838,992	14,311,114
8,962,163	14,788,117	17,251,244	9,233,198	13,084,277	14,676,916
8,980,358	15,139,289	17,883,309	9,207,827	13,309,355	15,057,314
8,985,460	15,492,578	18,543,373	9,165,025	13,536,491	15,453,176
8,976,336	15,847,692	19,233,623	9,103,360	13,765,391	15,865,476
8,951,776	16,204,325	19,952,528	9,031,369	13,995,803	16,314,839

For Ken and Kathy, using their taxable account to pay the tax bill meant that the breakeven point was thirteen years. This means that paying tax on the seeds took thirteen years to make sense. From that point forward, it was beneficial for them from a net worth point of view. Net worth does not equal income. Net worth, in this example, just means that if Ken and Kathy were to take all their money out of all their accounts, paying any tax due at the time, their net worth would be $8,627,166 if they did not convert. By converting, their net worth would be $8,629,292. It's not a lot at that point in time, but it is just one measurement of whether it makes sense to convert or not.

For Ken and Kathy, the conversion made sense from the perspective of more net worth for them while they are alive and also more after-tax value going to their children upon their death. But that was not the deciding factor. The real reason it made sense to them was that it eliminated their yearly income tax bill. We could get them to the point of *zero* percent tax rates.

Chapter 6

Understanding Required Minimum Distributions

Ken and Kathy are not unlike many retirees who have been good stewards of their money. They have made smart choices and saved over their lifetime in order to be in a position to enjoy the retirement they envisioned. For many people, until the day actually arrives, it is hard to picture what retirement really looks like. When Ken and Kathy sat down with the advisor, he went through their income and explained how he was going to create the income they needed during their retirement. During that conversation, he explained to Ken and Kathy that once they turned seventy-two, the IRS was going to require them to take money out of their retirement accounts, even if they didn't need the income.

Let's take a minute and ponder what that looks like in real terms.

- You are being forced to take withdrawals from your retirement savings even if you don't want or need the money.
- You have made all the sacrifices to save the money.
- You have paid all the fees (hidden or otherwise).
- You have taken all the risks associated with the investments.

Yes, you did get a tax break for saving in your retirement accounts, and because of that, the IRS now wants their share of your hard-earned money.

Adding insult to injury are the news reports of different groups scamming and taking advantage of retirees: identity theft, pending lawsuit claims, Social Security impersonation, romance scams, "calls from grandchildren in trouble" scams, computer support scams, "winning the lottery" scams, IRS collection scams, and the list goes on. The one that nobody actually mentions? The required minimum distribution (RMD) scam.

Did you know that if you fail to file a return, your tax penalty is up to 25 percent? That is right. If you just don't file your returns each year, your penalty is up to 25 percent. Filing your taxes but not paying? That penalty is only 1/2 percent per month. What is the penalty for not taking enough money out of your retirement accounts each year? *Fifty percent!* That is right: not making the correct RMD calculation and correct withdrawals is a 50-percent penalty (*plus*, you still have to pay the tax). Imagine this scenario:

RMD amount	$2,000.00
Penalty (50%)	$1,000.00
Tax (22%)	$ 440.00

Out of your $2,000 required minimum distribution of $2,000, you lose 72 percent to taxes. Plus, don't forget the state and local income tax that might be added just for good measure! To make matters worse, the IRS doesn't make the RMD calculation easy. Every year the numbers change. To calculate your RMD, you must first start with the 12/31 balance of your retirement accounts from the prior year. For example, in 2021, you will calculate the amount you must withdraw based upon the 12/31/2020 account values. That seems easy enough.

The next step is a little trickier. You must then go to the IRS lifetime tables—*tables, plural!* There is one table for you and another table if you are married and your spouse is ten years younger than you. There is yet another table for non-spouse beneficiaries that in itself has three different options and calculations. The IRS couldn't just make it simple and require that you take a simple percentage every year. Nope. They change the percentage each year.

To further complicate the rules, you must take RMDs from each category of retirement account you own: IRA, 401(k), 403(b), 457, profit sharing, etc. But wait—it gets even more complicated. Let's say you have

IRAs at three banks and two 401(k)s—one from the company from which you just retired and one from an old job. You must calculate your RMDs for each of the accounts individually. You can then take the RMD requirement from a single account, but only if the single account is like the other accounts. Huh?

Your investment company may issue you an IRS Form 5498 or otherwise calculate your RMDs on your behalf. Please note that the 5498 does come with a disclosure about consulting with a tax advisor to make sure your calculations are done correctly.

For example, let's assume you have the following three IRAs:

Bank #1	$20,000.00
Bank #2	30,000.00
Bank #3	50,000.00
Total IRA values 12/31	$100,000.00

In addition, let's also assume you have the following 401(k)s:

Job #1	$300,000
Job #2	$100,000
Total 401(k) values 12/31	$400,000

Uniform Lifetime Table

Age	Life Expectancy Factor	Age	Life Expectancy Factor
70	27.4	82	17.1
71	26.5	83	16.3
72	25.6	84	15.5
73	24.7	85	14.8
74	23.8	86	14.1
75	22.9	87	13.4
76	22.0	88	12.7
77	21.2	89	12.0
78	20.3	90	11.4
79	19.5	91	10.8
80	18.7	92	10.2
81	17.9	93	9.6

The older you get, the greater the percentage you are required to take out of your retirement accounts. At age seventy-two, the RMD is just over 3.9 percent. By the time you reach age ninety, that percentage is just under 9 percent. If you happen to make it to one hundred years old, you are being forced to withdraw almost 16 percent per year.

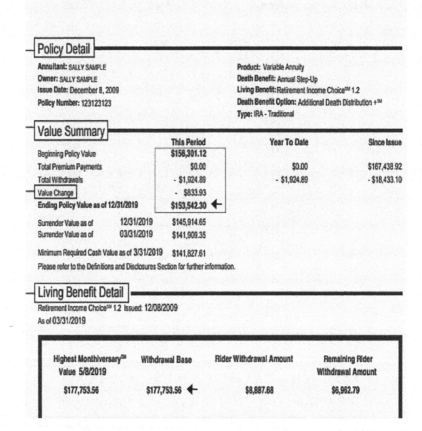

SALLY SAMPLE
4333 EDGEWOOD ROAD NE
CEDAR RAPIDS IA 52499

Policy Detail

Annuitant: SALLY SAMPLE
Owner: SALLY SAMPLE
Issue Date: December 8, 2009
Policy Number: 123123123

Product: Variable Annuity
Death Benefit: Annual Step-Up
Living Benefit: Retirement Income Choice℠ 1.2
Death Benefit Option: Additional Death Distribution +℠
Type: IRA - Traditional

Value Summary

	This Period	Year To Date	Since Issue
Beginning Policy Value	$156,301.12		
Total Premium Payments	$0.00	$0.00	$167,438.92
Total Withdrawals	- $1,924.89	- $1,924.89	- $18,433.10
Value Change	- $833.93		
Ending Policy Value as of 12/31/2019	$153,542.30 ←		
Surrender Value as of	12/31/2019	$145,914.65	
Surrender Value as of	03/31/2019	$141,909.35	

Minimum Required Cash Value as of 3/31/2019 $141,827.61

Please refer to the Definitions and Disclosures Section for further information.

Living Benefit Detail

Retirement Income Choice℠ 1.2 Issued: 12/08/2009
As of 03/31/2019

Highest Monthiversary℠ Value 5/8/2019	Withdrawal Base	Rider Withdrawal Amount	Remaining Rider Withdrawal Amount
$177,753.56	$177,753.56 ←	$8,887.68	$6,962.79

If you happen to own an annuity with an income rider benefit, the RMD calculations could be based upon the future value of those payments. In addition, taking income benefit withdrawals does **not** satisfy RMD requirements for your retirement accounts. **And**, if you do own an annuity, not only is the RMD calculated differently, but you could also lose the rider value if your RMDs are greater than the amount the annuity will produce. You need to talk to a professional about taxes before you commit to an annuity with an income rider.

RMDs sound confusing, don't they? In this example, if the total value of your IRAs is $100,000, your total aged seventy-two RMD on those three accounts is just about $3,906. You can choose to take that amount from any combination of the three IRAs, including taking it all from one of the IRAs. What you can't do is take that dollar amount from your 401(k)s.

The RMD on the $400,000 of 401(k) money equals $15,624.00. Just like the IRA accounts, you can choose to take the total 401(k) RMD amount from one or both 401(k)s. As long as you get the total amount out, the IRS does not care from which 401(k) it comes. You just can't take the 401(k) RMDs from an IRA.

Sounds complicated. But the IRS also threw another rule into the mix. If you are still working and still eligible (notice the word "eligible," which is not necessarily contributing) to contribute to your company's 401(k) plan, then you do not have an RMD requirement at all. No RMDs are required from your company-sponsored retirement plans while you are still working and eligible to contribute, even after you reach age seventy.

The IRS sure didn't make this rule easy. It almost feels like they made it so complicated just so they could confuse people, especially as they get older so that the IRS could collect penalties on incorrect RMD calculations.

Fortunately for Ken and Kathy, their investment advisor suggested that they work with their CPA each year to make sure they were calculating their RMDs correctly. Fortunately for Ken and Kathy, they had accumulated enough assets that they really didn't need their retirement accounts to fund their retirement. And fortunately for Ken and Kathy, they decided to work with a financial planning team that incorporated tax planning into the process. It was during that process that Ken and Kathy remembered that, for a short period of time, before they had kids, Kathy worked for a local hospital as a nurse. While working there, she contributed to her 403(b), and like many employees, she took a "set it and forget it" approach to the retirement account.

When Ken and Kathy had their tax analysis done to determine whether it made sense to convert some portion of their retirement accounts into Roth IRAs, it was discovered that they had never taken their RMDs from the 403(b) annuity Kathy had through the hospital. After a quick calculation, it was determined that she had failed to withdraw $12,845 over the previous three years. The penalty, according to her CPA, was $6,422.50 plus a tax bill of $2,747, for a whopping total of $9,169 in penalties and taxes.

Part IX	Additional Tax on Excess Accumulation in Qualified Retirement Plans (Including IRAs). Complete this part if you did not receive the minimum required distribution from your qualified retirement plan.		
52	Minimum required distribution for 2019 (see instructions)	**52**	
53	Amount actually distributed to you in 2019	**53**	
54	Subtract line 53 from line 52. If zero or less, enter -0-	**54**	
55	Additional tax. Enter 50% (0.50) of line 54. Include this amount on Schedule 2 (Form 1040 or 1040-SR), line 6, or Form 1040-NR, line 57	**55**	
Sign Here Only if You Are Filing This Form by Itself and Not With Your Tax Return	Under penalties of perjury, I declare that I have examined this form, including accompanying attachments, and to the best of my knowledge and belief, it is true, correct, and complete. Declaration of preparer (other than taxpayer) is based on all information of which preparer has any knowledge.		
	▶ Your signature	▶ Date	

The solution for Ken and Kathy was to request an abatement, or a waiver, of the IRS penalty. Their CPA had failed to make this request, probably because Ken and Kathy just handed her a 1099 from the hospital, and the CPA didn't take any time to review the problem. She just put numbers on a page—you know, like a historian. We were able to get the IRS to waive the penalty and save the client the $6,422.50 they had already paid.

This is why tax planning matters!

What counts as truly tax free? We have discussed the use of a Roth and/or a Roth 401(k) extensively. There is one other tax-free option for people. If you have a weak stomach or are easily frightened, you may want to skip this next approach to tax planning. Most ranking articles out there put members of Congress, politicians, and lawyers at the bottom of the "trustworthy" list. Used car salespeople are frequently on that list. So are life insurance agents. Many people assume the only reason an agent sells life insurance is to get the commission associated with selling insurance. It may be true. Life insurance agents do get paid a commission when they sell a life policy. Frequently, agents don't understand the policy they are selling, misrepresent how the policy works, and sell insurance to people who really don't benefit from the coverage. All that adds to the negative perception of life insurance. This doesn't mean that properly structured life insurance can't be a viable tool, especially when it comes to tax planning.

Remember our builder who sold his company for $4,125,000? His CPA had done the tax calculations and had given the contractor estimated tax payment coupons so he could send the IRS $1,000,000. That was the recommendation of the CPA—the person who the builder trusted to give him the best tax-planning advice—"Send in a check."

Form **1040**	Department of the Treasury—Internal Revenue Service (99) **U.S. Individual Income Tax Return**	**2020**	OMB No. 1545-0074	IRS Use Only—Do not write or staple in this space.

| **Filing Status** Check only one box. | [X] Single ☐ Married filing jointly ☐ Married filing separately (MFS) ☐ Head of household (HOH) ☐ Qualifying widow(er) (QW) If you checked the MFS box, enter the name of your spouse. If you checked the HOH or QW box, enter the child's name if the qualifying person is a child but not your dependent ▶ |

Your first name and middle initial	Last name		Your social security number
BOB	BUILDER		123-45-6789
If joint return, spouse's first name and middle initial	Last name		Spouse's social security number

Home address (number and street). If you have a P.O. box, see instructions.		Apt. no.	**Presidential Election Campaign** Check here if you, or your spouse if filing jointly, want $3 to go to this fund. Checking a box below will not change your tax or refund. ☐ You ☐ Spouse
123 Your Street			
City, town, or post office. If you have a foreign address, also complete spaces below.	State	ZIP code	
Foreign country name	Foreign province/state/county	Foreign postal code	

At any time during 2020, did you receive, sell, send, exchange, or otherwise acquire any financial interest in any virtual currency? ☐ Yes ☐ No

Standard Deduction	Someone can claim: ☐ You as a dependent ☐ Your spouse as a dependent ☐ Spouse itemizes on a separate return or you were a dual-status alien

Age/Blindness	You: [X] Were born before January 2, 1956 ☐ Are blind Spouse: [X] Was born before January 2, 1956 ☐ Is blind

Dependents (see instructions): If more than four dependents, see instructions and check here ▶ ☐	(1) First name Last name	(2) Social security number	(3) Relationship to you	(4) ✓ if qualifies for (see instructions): Child tax credit / Credit for other dependents

	1	Wages, salaries, tips, etc. Attach Form(s) W-2			1	
Attach Sch. B if required.	2a	Tax-exempt interest	2a	b Taxable interest	2b	14,282
	3a	Qualified dividends	3a 88,479	b Ordinary dividends	3b	14,262
	4a	IRA distributions	4a 42,000	b Taxable amount	4b	32,000
	5a	Pensions and annuities	5a	b Taxable amount	5b	
Standard Deduction for—	6a	Social security benefits	6a 79,500	b Taxable amount	6b	67,575
• Single or Married filing separately, $12,400	7	Capital gain or (loss). Attach Schedule D if required. If not required, check here ▶ ☐			7	4,236,202
	8	Other income from Schedule 1, line 9			8	
• Married filing jointly or Qualifying widow(er), $24,800	9	Add lines 1, 2b, 3b, 4b, 5b, 6b, 7, and 8. This is your total income ▶			9	4,364,321
	10	Adjustments to income:				
	a	From Schedule 1, line 22		10a		
• Head of household, $18,650	b	Charitable contributions if you take the standard deduction. See instructions		10b		
	c	Add lines 10a and 10b. These are your total adjustments to income ▶			10c	
• If you checked any box under Standard Deduction, see instructions.	11	Subtract line 10c from line 9. This is your adjusted gross income ▶			11	4,364,321
	12	Standard deduction or itemized deductions (from Schedule A)			12	15,700
	13	Qualified business income deduction. Attach Form 8995 or Form 8995-A			13	0
	14	Add lines 12 and 13			14	15,700
	15	Taxable income. Subtract line 14 from line 11. If zero or less, enter -0-			15	4,348,621

Includes $4.125M from the sale.

Form 1040 (2020)	BOB BUILDER		123-45-6789		**Page 2**

16	Tax (see instructions). Check if any from Form(s): 1 ☐ 8814 2 ☐ 4972 3 ☐ _____			16	844,326
17	Amount from Schedule 2, line 3			17	7,632
18	Add lines 16 and 17			18	851,958
19	Child tax credit or credit for other dependents			19	
20	Amount from Schedule 3, line 7			20	
21	Add lines 19 and 20			21	
22	Subtract line 21 from line 18. If zero or less, enter -0-			22	851,958
23	Other taxes, including self-employment tax, from Schedule 2, line 10			23	158,244
24	Add lines 22 and 23. This is your total tax ▶			24	1,010,202
25	Federal income tax withheld from:				

Notice the total tax due? Line 24? Over $1 million! Yep. "Just pay it" was the advice.

Because tax planning matters, we created a different solution for Bob and Kim. Remember that they had made smart money choices along the way and had an ample retirement and investment portfolio to meet most of their needs. The sale of the practice would fund their legacy planning and charitable giving and help off-set those bucket list and get-around-to-it items. What was the solution? Life insurance—properly designed cash-value life insurance. The operative words here are "properly designed."

When properly designing a life insurance contract, you need to understand *the goal of the policy*. For some people, the goal is to protect their family should they die with young children and replace the lost income. For some, it is to pay off debt related to a mortgage. For others, it is to leave a legacy; that is, to make somebody "rich." For Bob and Kim, the goal was threefold: first, they wanted to leave a legacy for the kids; second, they wanted to contribute to their favorite charities; and third, they wanted to reduce their tax exposure.

The first step was to attack the current tax bill. The CPA had calculated that $1,010,202 tax bill. The solution for reducing this tax bite was for Bob and Kim to donate $1 million to a specific type of charitable trust. This allowed them to immediately write off $1 million as a tax deduction. With this simple step, he was able to reduce his taxable income by $1 million. That, in turn, saved him over $200,000 in taxes.

Form **1040**	Department of the Treasury—Internal Revenue Service (99)		**2020**	OMB No. 1545-0074	IRS Use Only—Do not write or staple in this space.

Filing Status
Check only one box.

[X] Single [ ] Married filing jointly [ ] Married filing separately (MFS) [ ] Head of household (HOH) [ ] Qualifying widow(er) (QW)
If you checked the MFS box, enter the name of your spouse. If you checked the HOH or QW box, enter the child's name if the qualifying person is a child but not your dependent ▶

Your first name and middle initial	Last name	Your social security number
BOB	BUILDER	123-45-6789
If joint return, spouse's first name and middle initial	Last name	Spouse's social security number

Home address (number and street). If you have a P.O. box, see instructions. **123 Your Street** — Apt. no.

City, town, or post office. If you have a foreign address, also complete spaces below. — State — ZIP code

Foreign country name — Foreign province/state/county — Foreign postal code

Presidential Election Campaign
Check here if you, or your spouse if filing jointly, want $3 to go to this fund. Checking a box below will not change your tax or refund. [ ] You [ ] Spouse

At any time during 2020, did you receive, sell, send, exchange, or otherwise acquire any financial interest in any virtual currency? [ ] Yes [ ] No

Standard Deduction
Someone can claim: [ ] You as a dependent [ ] Your spouse as a dependent
[ ] Spouse itemizes on a separate return or you were a dual-status alien

Age/Blindness You: [X] Were born before January 2, 1956 [ ] Are blind Spouse: [X] Was born before January 2, 1956 [ ] Is blind

Dependents (see instructions):

(1) First name Last name	(2) Social security number	(3) Relationship to you	(4) ✓ if qualifies for (see instructions): Child tax credit	Credit for other dependents
			[ ]	[ ]
			[ ]	[ ]
			[ ]	[ ]
			[ ]	[ ]

If more than four dependents, see instructions and check here ▶ [ ]

Attach Sch. B if required.

1	Wages, salaries, tips, etc. Attach Form(s) W-2		**1**	14,282
2a	Tax-exempt interest	2a	b Taxable interest **2b**	14,262
3a	Qualified dividends	3a 88,479	b Ordinary dividends **3b**	32,000
4a	IRA distributions	4a 42,000	b Taxable amount **4b**	
5a	Pensions and annuities	5a	b Taxable amount **5b**	
6a	Social security benefits	6a 79,500	b Taxable amount **6b**	67,575
7	Capital gain or (loss). Attach Schedule D if required. If not required, check here . . . . ▶ [ ]		**7**	4,236,202
8	Other income from Schedule 1, line 9		**8**	
9	Add lines 1, 2b, 3b, 4b, 5b, 6b, 7, and 8. This is your total income . . . . ▶		**9**	4,364,321
10	Adjustments to income:			
a	From Schedule 1, line 22	10a		
b	Charitable contributions if you take the standard deduction. See instructions	10b		
c	Add lines 10a and 10b. These are your total adjustments to income . . . . ▶		**10c**	
11	Subtract line 10c from line 9. This is your adjusted gross income . . . . ▶		**11**	4,364,321
12	Standard deduction or itemized deductions (from Schedule A) . .		**12**	1,010,000
13	Qualified business income deduction. Attach Form 8995 or Form 8995-A		**13**	0
14	Add lines 12 and 13		**14**	1,010,000
15	Taxable income. Subtract line 14 from line 11. If zero or less, enter -0-		**15**	3,354,321

Form 1040 (2020)   BOB BUILDER   123-45-6789   Page 2

16	Tax (see instructions). Check if any from Form(s): 1 [ ] 8814 2 [ ] 4972 3 [ ] _____ . . .		**16**	642,792
17	Amount from Schedule 2, line 3		**17**	2,000
18	Add lines 16 and 17		**18**	644,792
19	Child tax credit or credit for other dependents		**19**	
20	Amount from Schedule 3, line 7		**20**	
21	Add lines 19 and 20		**21**	
22	Subtract line 21 from line 18. If zero or less, enter -0-		**22**	644,792
23	Other taxes, including self-employment tax, from Schedule 2, line 10		**23**	158,244
24	Add lines 22 and 23. This is your total tax . . . . ▶		**24**	803,036
25	Federal income tax withheld from:			
a	Form(s) W-2	25a		

The contribution immediately reduced their income by almost $1 million and they saved over $200,000 in taxes. And that was just the start.

The $1 million went into the charitable trust, and each year, a portion of the trust goes to their charities and a portion of the trust is used to fund a $1 million life insurance policy. They were able to accomplish two of their goals using one tax strategy: a lifetime of charitable giving and a legacy for the children. They were able to use what would have otherwise been spent on taxes to accomplish the goals. Every year they are able to donate more than $58,000 to charity (resulting in more tax deductions, by the way), and their kids get the $1 million that would have otherwise gone to pay taxes. That makes a difference, which is what their goals were: As a builder, he made a difference in his clients' lives, and as a retiree, he is still able to make a difference in people's lives.

That is why tax planning matters!

To further eliminate his tax bill, they used Section §1031 of the tax code to further reduce the tax bill to almost *zero*, resulting from the sale of the business. Section 1031 of the federal tax code allows you to avoid taxes on the sale of property otherwise subject to capital gains by taking the proceeds from the sale and investing in substantially the same type of property within a specified period of time. In the case of Bob and Kim, almost $3 million of the sales price they were receiving was related to the building where his construction company was housed.

16	Tax (see instructions). Check if any from Form(s): 1 ☐ 8814 2 ☐ 4972 3 ☐ _____ . . .			16	79,074
17	Amount from Schedule 2, line 3			17	
18	Add lines 16 and 17			18	79,074
19	Child tax credit or credit for other dependents			19	
20	Amount from Schedule 3, line 7			20	
21	Add lines 19 and 20			21	
22	Subtract line 21 from line 18. If zero or less, enter -0-			22	79,074
23	Other taxes, including self-employment tax, from Schedule 2, line 10			23	44,244
24	Add lines 22 and 23. This is your total tax . . . . ▶			24	123,318

Notice the tax difference? With proper tax planning in place, we were able to save Bob and Kim almost $900,000 in taxes—$900,000 in tax savings. "Cut a check for $1 million" was the advice given by the CPA and the investment advisor. Just pay the IRS.

Tax Planning Matters!

Using the tax code to eliminate their tax bill allowed them to use the full $3 million of the proceeds to generate $195,000 a year. And because of the way a 1031 can work, almost 40 percent of the income, or $80,000 of the income, was tax free. This was only the starting point for Bob and Kim. They liked the $190,000 income, but they wanted even more tax savings. Like many retirees, they didn't want to pay tax on their Social Security and quite frankly, they liked the idea of paying the least amount of tax legally possible. Certainly, that's something most of us strive to accomplish.

They wanted to get their tax bill down and were worried about what impact the RMDs would have on their collective Social Security at age seventy-two. The CPA had told them that 85 percent was going to be taxable and to just accept the fact that when you make considerable income, you have to pay considerable tax. We disagree. With proper planning, you can reduce and quite possibly eliminate your tax bill.

The next step in planning for Bob and Kim was to use life insurance—properly structured life insurance. For five years, they funded a properly designed life insurance policy. They took $162,500 of the income they were receiving from the 1031 exchange and added it to the proceeds from their IRA withdrawals. The goal was to almost deplete the IRA accounts completely by the time they reached age seventy-two. At the time of the sale of the company, Bob and Kim had about $1.5 million saved in their 401(k). At retirement, they rolled his 401(k), a tax-free transfer, into an IRA.

The goal was to leave about $300,000 in the IRA and deplete the balance over the course of five years. Strategically, they withdrew $250,000 each year. They paid the taxes out of his savings account. Remember from their return, he was earning almost $15,000 a year in interest and had just under $1 million in cash, earning almost nothing. It made better sense to pay taxes with those "lazy" dollars than to use their other investments that were making market returns. After taxes, combined with the 1031 income, they paid a premium into a properly designed life insurance policy, to the tune of $400,000 a year for the full five years.

What is a properly designed life insurance policy? A properly designed policy (sometimes called a LIRP, or life insurance retirement plan) allows a policy owner to fund the life policy for a set term of years. The policy grows based upon a contractually agreed-upon amount: it could be a fixed interest rate, a variable interest rate, or even participating in stock market returns. Based upon the returns and fewer fees associated with owning insurance, the policy will grow to a specified amount. The beauty of life insurance is that under IRS Code 7702(g), earnings in a life insurance policy are not taxable. Under IRC Section 72, any distributions are treated as a withdrawal of principal first. And finally, most life insurance contracts allow the owner of the policy to "borrow" money from the contract, and under IRC 7702 and IRC 72, such loans are not included in your taxable income. In simple English? We can get money out tax free!

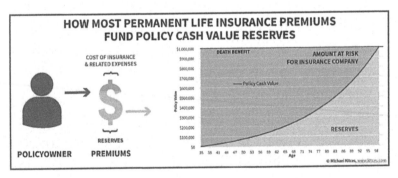

Their policy was designed to front-load the cash by making excessive premium payments in the amount of $400,000 per year for five years. This, in turn, would allow them to subsequently take tax-free withdrawals during their retirement.

Net After Tax Outlay	Annualized Surrender	Annualized Policy Loan	Annualized Loan Interest	Gross Cash Value	Total Outstanding Loan	Net Cash Value	Net Death Benefit	Reduced Paid-up Death Benefit
400,000	0	0	0	49,001	0	49,001	5,869,589	111,238
400,000	0	0	0	359,911	0	359,911	5,953,066	792,879
400,000	0	0	0	724,540	0	724,540	6,035,149	1,549,420
400,000	0	0	0	1,172,662	0	1,172,662	6,249,778	2,435,335
400,000	0	0	0	1,664,543	0	1,664,543	6,505,427	3,358,778
-162,000†	0	524,398	0	2,130,457	524,398	1,586,952	6,141,022	3,113,380
-162,000†	0	543,506	19,108	2,614,199	1,067,904	1,504,088	5,755,713	2,870,946
-162,000†	0	566,605	42,207	3,121,885	1,634,509	1,421,089	5,348,876	2,640,743
-162,000†	0	590,686	66,287	3,656,391	2,225,195	1,339,805	4,924,460	2,425,295
-162,000†	0	615,790	91,391	4,220,739	2,840,984	1,262,192	4,485,964	2,226,796
-162,000†	0	279,563	117,563	4,444,533	3,120,547	1,194,542	4,388,734	2,054,773
-162,000†	0	291,444	129,444	4,674,991	3,411,991	1,121,170	4,280,349	1,881,095
-162,000†	0	303,830	141,830	4,906,671	3,715,821	1,036,107	4,160,471	1,696,117
-162,000†	0	316,743	154,743	5,151,435	4,032,564	950,667	4,029,103	1,519,098
-162,000†	0	330,205	168,205	5,403,786	4,362,769	858,779	3,886,021	1,340,147
-162,000†	0	344,238	182,238	5,735,824	4,707,007	831,948	3,841,202	1,268,833
-162,000†	0	358,868	196,868	6,088,930	5,065,875	810,934	3,799,213	1,209,574
-162,000†	0	374,120	212,120	6,463,712	5,439,996	795,696	3,759,030	1,161,414
-162,000†	0	390,020	228,020	6,855,050	5,830,016	780,437	3,720,034	1,115,389
-162,000†	0	406,596	244,596	7,274,989	6,236,613	776,499	3,681,237	1,087,230

> The policy was designed for them to make five payments of $400,000. In the sixth year, they were able to withdraw $162,000 a year tax free!

By designing the policy correctly, the cash value was maximized to provide tax-free income to Bob and Kim, and the death benefit was reduced down to the smallest amount possible while allowing the policy to still distribute the $162,000 to the two of them. With a life expectancy of ninety years of age, they will have invested approximately $2 million into the policy. Upon the survivor's death at age ninety, between the two of them, they will have withdrawn over $3.8 million tax free, and still have a death benefit of over $1.1 million going to their heirs.

It is important to understand how the cash values, death benefits, and policy loans all work together to ensure that you don't end up violating IRC Sections 7702 and 72, which would result in everything unraveling and a huge tax bill.

That is why tax planning matters!

When a well-planned, tax-efficient retirement plan comes together:

Income:	
Social Security	$79,500
Dividends and Interest	19,721
LIRP	162,500
IRA Distributions	9,949
Capital Gains	32,250
Total Income	$303,920
Taxes: *Zero! None! Nothing!*	

Remember that the LIRP, $162,000, is not taxable. Also remember that they are charitable minded and that is the bulk of their itemized deductions.

Notice their tax bill? *Zero!*

So what happens to Bob and Kim when the taxes rates go up, like so many have predicted they will?

If taxes rates double in the future, they still remain in the zero percent tax bracket.

Tax planning matters!

The Secure Act of 2019

On December 20, 2019, President Trump signed the Secure Act into law. The changes contained in the Act may have an impact on your retirement plan, but they most certainly will have an impact on your tax-planning choices.

Here are a few key takeaways to consider:

1. **Required Minimum Distributions:** We discussed those pesky RMDs, and with the Secure Act, you have a little breathing room regarding when you are required to start taking your distributions and giving one-third of your proceeds to the IRS. Remember, at age seventy and a half, you would be forced to take a distribution from your retirement accounts. You had to take this money out each and every year, regardless of whether you would need it or not. You had all those crazy calculations on all those different accounts, and if you missed something (even if it was unintentional), the IRS penalized you 50 percent—*plus*, they wanted the taxes.

   What has changed is that you no longer have to take money out of your retirement accounts by age seventy and a half. Now you have to take the money out by age seventy-two. You basically get a one-and-one-half-year postponement of your RMDs. This could provide a key cushion when it comes to your income needs, especially if your first RMD would have been due in a year when the stock markets were in decline. While there is a small positive from this, all the other issues remain: which account to take the distribution from, what percentage to take, how to calculate on the various investment accounts, and all the other issues that arise when trying to avoid the 50 percent penalty.

2. **Contribution Age Limits:** With the Secure Act in place, for those who work past the age of seventy, you are allowed to contribute to your IRA, even if you are otherwise required to take an RMD. With Americans living and working longer, this can be a huge boost. You will still have RMDs, but if you move your existing IRAs into your existing 401(k)s, you may not be subject to much of an RMD at all.

And remember, if you have a spouse who is retired, you will now be able to contribute to their IRAs. You can still use this contribution to create a "back-door" Roth contribution if your income otherwise prevents a direct contribution to a Roth.

Part-Time Coverage: If you do choose to continue working past age seventy-two, when RMDs now come into play, you may be eligible to participate in your company's 401(k) plan. The problem is that in the past, you probably had to work at least a certain number of hours per year in order to qualify for participation. For many plans, this required you to work at least 1,000 hours per year. Not hard to do if you choose to work twenty hours per week all year. For many of those who want to continue to work in some capacity, those hours might be hard to hit. Under the Secure Act, the new rule provides for participation with just 500 hours a year, which is about ten hours per week. Remember, your ability to participate in your company's plan is key to avoiding current-year RMDs.

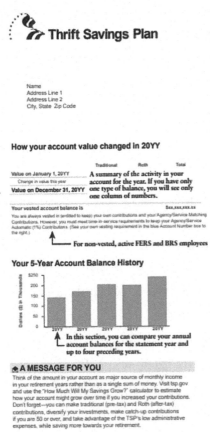

One of the new rules is actually quite interesting and could cause incredible problems in the investment world.

For insurance agents and financial advisors who sell annuities with income riders as part of their practice, the new rule requiring 401(k) plan administrators to show on the 401(k) statement how much a participant could receive if the total account balance was used to purchase an annuity is a validation of their long-held belief that if you need income during retirement, an annuity is a viable tool.

The problem is that most firms and insurance companies that provide annuities have an unwritten guideline, a rule, that limits the amount of money an advisor can actually put into an annuity on behalf of their client. For many firms and advisors, no more than 50 percent of the client's investments should be held in an annuity.

Lifetime Income Disclosure Statements

The regulatory agency for security-licensed advisors is called FINRA (the Financial Industry Regulatory Authority). They provide a guidebook to investors who are considering using annuities:

https://www.finra.org/investors/ insights/
your-guide-annuities-introduction.

For insurance agents, the National Association of
Insurance Commissioners (the state insurance commissioners) has also produced a guidebook that might
prove useful in your research:

https://www.naic.org/documents/prod_serv_
consumer_anb_ la.pdf.

The idea here is that the 401(k) participant uses the
value of their 401(k) to produce income. This makes
sense because, for the most part, people who put money away into their employer retirement accounts typically do so to save for their retirement. For them, the
goal is to save enough money in these accounts so that
when they retire, they have enough income to enjoy
their retirement years. So it makes sense that the 401(k)
administrators should tell their participants how much
they could expect to receive if they took income from
their retirement plans.

The concern about this new feature, showing the
possible income for the participant, is that the income
is based upon what is called a SPIA: a single premium
immediate annuity. This means that the number shown
in our example ($1,263 per month) is for the life of
just the participant. It is based upon a single life, which
means that if you are married, your spouse would not
get any income or have any assets available from the
plan should you die first. That's right—once you pass
away, the income is gone. You have basically turned the

value of the retirement plan over to an insurance company, and they, in turn, have guaranteed *you* a lifetime of income. If you live to be a hundred years old, you did great. If you get hit by that proverbial pickle truck the day after your first check, nothing is left. *Zero.* Nothing. It is gone. Now, you will probably have options about whether to put the whole amount into an annuity, take a single life policy and get the maximum value out of the amount, or provide for your spouse and receive a lesser amount. The choices will be similar to those you have with a company-sponsored pension plan. The options are almost overwhelming, and you will need to pay attention so that you do not inadvertently cut off your spouse or heirs.

Other Provisions: These include (a) allowing grad students to use their stipends and grants to qualify as income for contribution purposes; (b) foster care providers and adult caregivers will also have opportunities to contribute based upon their payments, (c) employers will now offer "automatic" enrollment to employees, requiring employees to opt out of saving for retirement, and (d) incentives for small businesses to set up plans for their employees.

As always, there can't only be good news, right?

Stretch Provisions Eliminated: As previously discussed, any assets left inside a retirement account left to a spouse had one set of rules related to required minimum distributions. Basically, the spouse was allowed to continue taking the RMDs based upon their age when they inherited the account. For children and other heirs, there was a different lifetime table, but effectively they were also able to stretch that amount left in the retirement account over their own lifetimes.

This is important because many heirs are in their peak earning years, and they may not want to be forced to take out more income from their inherited IRAs. It only forces them to pay more taxes on money they don't really need at this point. Sound familiar? One of the many reasons to consider converting to a Roth IRA, right?

Well, perhaps. The new rule eliminates the ability of a non-spouse beneficiary to stretch out those withdrawals over their lifetime. This means that non-spouse heirs will no longer be allowed to stretch out those withdrawals, which means that those tax-free or tax-deferred accounts are not able to grow tax free or tax deferred over their lives. They lose the ability to let those accounts grow for decades without having to pay tax on any current tax on potential growth.

With few exceptions, nonspousal beneficiaries are now required to withdraw 100 percent of the inherited account within ten years. This means that if you have an IRA, your heirs will have to take 100 percent of that money out, add it to their own current income, and pay taxes on it—each and every year for up to ten years. This is a huge loss of potential tax-free growth and income for your heirs.

The potential issue is even more drastic for many employer-sponsored plans, such as 401(k)s, 403(b)s, and the like. Many of those plans require that your non-spousal beneficiary withdraw 100 percent of the plan within five years. Think about how large that tax bill could be for your children and/or your heirs.

With every problem comes potential solutions. The changes to the stretch accounts are no different. Clearly, the conversion to a Roth IRA is now more important than ever. While it is true that an *inherited* Roth account has the same ten-year withdrawal requirement, at least those withdrawals are tax free. With proper tax planning during the withdrawal period, those Roth assets can be converted into either tax-free assets for the future or into tax-efficient assets in the future.

Tax efficient? Think about our Warren Buffet approach. Upon the withdrawal of the Roth assets, if your heir were to invest those in assets that produce only capital gains, then your heir could have that growth and dividend income exposed to favorable tax rates. Remember, if structured correctly, capital gains rates can be as low as *zero*. That is correct: The benefit of having a Roth is that any withdrawal results in *zero* taxes. The same can be true if your heirs properly structure their Roth withdrawals.

While we think the Warren Buffet approach to capital gains and taxes is important (remember, capital gains are currently taxed between 0 percent and 20 percent, while ordinary income is taxed up to almost 40 percent when you include the additional Medicare taxes), the reality is that they can change the capital gains rates, as we have seen over the last couple of decades (capital gains rates have been as high as 28 percent and as low as 0 percent over the last twenty years). What hasn't changed in decades is the ability to receive tax-free income from properly structured life insurance.

That means while tax efficient is good, tax free is even better. The whole purpose of the Roth IRA was to allow your beneficiaries (assumed to be your children) to take the balance of that inherited account over their lifetime. Let's say you have managed to accumulate $1 million in a Roth account. Under the old rules, when your daughter Susie inherited that account upon your death, she was allowed to take the $1 million out over her lifetime, about 5 percent per year. This allowed the money to continue to grow tax free while still providing income for her. If your daughter died with money left in that Roth account, her kids were allowed to continue taking that money out tax free. It was a wonderful tax-planning strategy.

At first glance, it appears that the Secure Act has taken away the ability to continue tax-free growth for heirs. The Secure Act requires your nonspousal beneficiary to withdraw 100 percent of the Roth account or IRA by the end of ten years. In doing so, it forces the money in that Roth or IRA out of tax-deferred growth and into an account that would be subject to minimal capital gains tax.

But with a little tax planning, your beneficiaries can continue to grow their inheritance tax free and create tax-free income. Remember, Susie was forced to take the required minimum distributions from the Roth (i.e., creating income). Now, instead of taking 5 percent (or deferring the whole thing for ten years and taking a lump sum), what if she took out 10 percent each and purchased a life insurance policy?

Let's take a look at that $1 million Roth IRA. Let's assume a few things: Your daughter inherits the Roth at age fifty and wants to retire at age sixty. She will need income during retirement, so she will take the money out of the Roth over seven years (we'll explain later why seven years is key), the money grows at 5 percent, and combined federal and state tax rates are at 22 percent.

When Susie takes her withdrawal every year, she will be putting the money into an investment account and be required to pay taxes on her capital gains and dividends each year. If she were to inherit the $1 million from your Roth IRA and take $164,590 per year for seven years and earn 5 percent on her investments, then her account would have grown to about $1.63 million after taxes. Taking this tax-efficient approach, she would be able to withdraw about $7,750 a month for thirty years and have nothing left for her heirs.

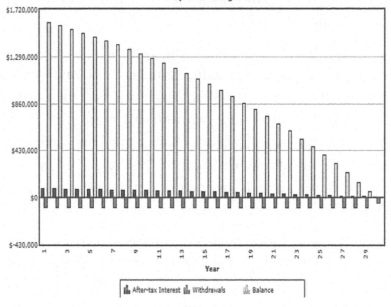

Lump Sum Savings Detail

Year

After-tax Interest | Withdrawals | Balance

> **HOW LONG WILL MY MONEY LAST WITH SYSTEMATIC WITHDRAWALS?**
> Starting balance: $1,630,000
> Rate of return: 5 percent
> Tax bracket: 22 percent
> Yearly distributions: Total distributions over thirty years will be approximately $2.75 million

Sounds pretty reasonable. Susie is able to supplement her income needs for thirty years with an additional income of $7,750 a month. That seems pretty tax efficient.

Perhaps a better approach would be using a tax-free strategy. Making the exact same assumptions, Susie could increase her income to $10,178 per month *tax free* and still have $1.2 million available to her heirs, also tax free. You're probably asking yourself, *how is that possible?*

Susie chose to use the Ed Slott approach to retirement planning by choosing to use the benefits of life insurance. By taking the same $164,590 withdrawals as before, Susie put those tax-free proceeds into a properly designed life insurance contract. She took the same seven years of withdrawals, and each and every year, she "invested" in her life insurance contract instead of the stock market via her brokerage account. The benefit here is that Susie adds no risk to her investments—since a properly designed life insurance policy does not expose her to stock market volatility. In addition to the removal of the ups and downs of the stock market, she is also sheltered from paying taxes on her dividends and capital gains. In properly structured life insurance, there are no taxes on any gains, dividends, or interest.

In order for life insurance to be properly structured, you must do a few important things. First, you must fund your life insurance premiums in such a fashion to avoid what is called an MEC, a modified endowment contract. In the simplest terms, an MEC translates into "taxable" when you take withdrawals from your insurance contract. With a properly structured contract, you can always "borrow" the gains and withdraw the principal. Borrowed money is never taxable, and neither is your principal. You must also use a policy that is designed to create income; that is, you want to maximize your income options and not necessarily your death benefit options.

In this scenario, the goal of Susie's parents was for Susie to have the money to use over her lifetime. Susie didn't need the money until she retired at age sixty, so being forced to take all the money out of the Roth IRA isn't really in her best interests, but with the new Secure Act rules, she must make sure the inherited Roth is drained of all assets by the end of ten years.

End of Year	Beg/ End of Yr Age	Annualized Annual Premium	Dist. Amount
1	50/51	$164,590.00	$0
2	51/52	$164,590.00	$0
3	52/53	$164,590.00	$0
4	53/54	$164,590.00	$0
5	54/55	$164,590.00	$0
		$822,950.00	$0
6	55/56	$164,590.00	$0
7	56/57	$164,590.00	$0
8	57/58	$0.00	$0
9	58/59	$0.00	$0
10	59/60	$0.00	$0
		$1,152,130.00	$0
11	60/61	$0.00	$122,136
12	61/62	$0.00	$122,136
13	62/63	$0.00	$122,136
14	63/64	$0.00	$122,136
15	64/65	$0.00	$122,136

In this illustration, you can see that Susie took her $164,590 per year and paid the premium on the properly structured cash-value life insurance policy. At age sixty, when Susie is ready to retire, she can start taking $122,136 a year out to supplement her income. In addition to the *lifetime* income provided by this properly designed life insurance, like all life insurance, there is a death benefit for Susie's heirs.

With this tax-efficient approach, at the end of ten years, Susie had about $1.625 million to leave to her heirs should she die unexpectedly. By using the tax-free approach, if Susie were to die unexpectedly at age sixty, she would be leaving her heirs slightly more than $4.1 million. And keep in mind that the money she is leaving is 100 percent tax free as well.

You can see that the death benefit decreases after the tenth year. Why? That is because Susie started taking her tax-free withdrawals of $122,000 per year. Just like withdrawals in her brokerage account would result in depleting the account over time, taking withdrawals from her life insurance policy will have similar consequences. The difference is that with the properly designed life insurance, Susie will have tax-free income—plus when she passes away, there is still a substantial legacy.

Notice below that by the time Susie dies at age ninety, she will have withdrawn over $3.6 million from her policy and still left a legacy of the original $1 million she inherited from the Roth IRA forty years ago!

Clearly, tax planning matters!

Account Value	Surrender Value	Death Benefit
$143,848	$0	$4,151,482
$294,746	$150,794	$4,151,482
$454,282	$317,906	$4,151,482
$624,057	$502,833	$4,151,482
$804,861	$698,791	$4,151,482
$997,552	$906,635	$4,151,482
$1,202,693	$1,126,928	$4,151,482
$1,253,494	$1,192,882	$4,151,482
$1,306,508	$1,261,049	$4,151,482
$1,361,941	$1,331,635	$4,151,482
$1,443,828	$1,318,097	$4,025,750
$1,530,406	$1,272,052	$3,893,128
$1,621,863	$1,223,619	$3,753,239
$1,720,283	$1,174,484	$3,605,683
$1,826,287	$1,124,847	$3,450,042

While using properly designed life insurance has been addressed in this book, more information on using life insurance as part of your tax-free retirement planning can be found in Patrick Kelly's national bestseller, *Tax-Free Retirement*. Retirement guru, CPA, and bestselling author, America's IRA Expert, Ed Slott's book, *The Retirement Savings Time Bomb . . . and How to Defuse It*, is a retirement guidebook for many tax professionals.

Tax planning does matter!

Chapter 7

Bonus Section: Small Business and Small Business Owners

In some of our examples, we talked about different kinds of income and professions. When thinking about workers, we sometimes think about the big tech, insurance, or retail companies.

However, the reality is that most people don't work for big corporate America. In fact, according to the Census Bureau, there are about 5.6 million employers in the United States, and almost all firms with fewer than twenty employees make up about 89 percent of those employers.[15] This means that the average American works for a small employer. These types of workers

---

15 https://sbecouncil.org/about-us/facts-and-data/

are the backbone of our economy, and thus they need a little extra attention when it comes to saving for taxes.

As individuals, small business owners and their employees can employ all the tax-planning strategies we have previously discussed. But there are a few other options and bits of information that the small business owner should consider:

o Many small business owners offer their employees the ability to participate in a company-sponsored retirement plan called a simplified employee pension, also known as an SEP IRA. An SEP IRA is a basic and simple way for an employer to contribute to their employee's retirement as well as to their own retirement plans.

They are simple because they are easy to open—as easy as opening an IRA—and because they have very simple rules for contributing to them:

- You must be twenty-one years old.

- You must have worked for the employer for at least three of the last five years.

- You must have earned at least $600 in compensation.

Once the SEP IRA has been established, you as an employer can contribute up to 25 percent of your profit into your own plan. The downside is that whatever percentage of your profit or salary you contribute to your own plan, you must make that much of a contribution to your employee's SEP plan.

All contributions are tax deductible for the employer. Note that the employee does not contribute to the SEP. The employee can, however, open their own IRA or Roth IRA and make contributions based upon their income level.

o An employer can also provide a 401(k) program for their employees: a defined contribution plan. It is called a defined contribution because the rules dictate how much can be contributed by the employee participant and the employer. The employee takes on the risk of success or failure in having the right amount of money saved to fund their retirement.

These plans are a little more complicated for the small business owner and require annual tax filing on IRS Form 5500. This form is required when a company-sponsored retirement plan has more than $500,000 in assets. This means as the retirement accounts grow in value over time, through market growth or contributions, you may be required to file additional tax forms for your company plan. A 401(k) can be a very creative solution to tax planning for very small firms of only two or three employees, including the owner and perhaps a spouse.

The costs of setting up the 401(k) and the annual administration can be intimidating at first. For example, hiring a third-party administrator to set up the plan may cost several thousand dollars. Annual reporting can cost just as much. Some payroll companies will offset the setup costs or waive them altogether.

The basic rules are as follows:

- The 401(k) can restrict participation to people who are older than twenty-one.

- The 401(k) can restrict when they can start participating—usually within a year of their hire date.

- Employees and employers can contribute 100 percent of their salary up to annual contribution limits: In 2020, those limits were $19,500 for those under age fifty, with an additional $6,500 catch up allowed for those fifty and over.

- The employer can set up a 401(k), a Roth 401(k), or both.

- Safe Harbor contributions avoid top-heavy testing.

- The 401(k) can provide profit sharing.

For the employer, especially a person who is the only "employee" of the firm, the amount that can be set aside is fairly substantial. However, if there are other employees involved, an employer will need to pass a "top-heavy" test: a test to make sure that the highly compensated aren't the only ones participating in the 401(k). The way around this rule is called a "safe harbor" provision, which requires the employer to match any contributions the employee makes. The match is typically dollar for dollar for the first 3 percent and then fifty cents per dollar for the next 2 percent. This basically means if the employee contributes 5 percent of their wages, the employer will need to contribute another 4 percent of the employee's wages to that employee's 401(k).

Jim's salary	$50,000
401(k) contribution (5 percent of his salary)	$2,500
Jim's W-2 taxable wages	$47,500

*This is a salary deferral and goes into Jim's 401(k). (If this is a Roth 401(k), there would be no reduction in Jim's taxable wages.) In addition to Jim's contribution, the employer would also be required to contribute $2,500 to Jim's 401(k) plan.

The real opportunity is in the case of a person who is the only full-time employee of the company. In another example, many doctors and dentists may have numerous nurses, practitioners, hygienists, and administrative help, but in many circumstances, those employees are not eligible to participate because of hours worked or income needs.

YOUR EMPLOYEE PRE-TAX DEFERRAL   Vesting = 100.00% / Your Vested Balance is $155,828.19

Fund Option	Beginning Balance	Contributions	Exchanges	Withdrawals	Gain/Loss	Adjustments	Closing Balance	Units
Balanced								
Vngrd Trgt Rtrmt 2025 Inv	$108,952.13	$5,731.28	$0.00	$0.00	$1,203.10	$3,126.45	$119,012.96	76,558.6528
Vngrd Trgt Rtrmt 2040 Inv	$587.39	$0.00	$0.00	$0.00	$2.49	$0.00	$589.88	356.0636
Sub Total	$109,539.52	$5,731.28	$0.00	$0.00	$1,205.59	$3,126.45	$119,602.84	
Outstanding Loan Balance							$36,225.35	
Total	$109,539.52	$5,731.28	$0.00	$0.00	$1,205.59	$3,126.45	$155,828.19	

YOUR EMPLOYER MATCHING   Vesting = 100.00% / Your Vested Balance is $30,148.12

Fund Option	Beginning Balance	Contributions	Exchanges	Withdrawals	Gain/Loss	Adjustments	Closing Balance	Units
Balanced								
Vngrd Trgt Rtrmt 2025 Inv	$28,577.77	$1,071.23	$0.00	$0.00	$304.86	$0.00	$29,953.86	19,268.7195
Vngrd Trgt Rtrmt 2040 Inv	$193.44	$0.00	$0.00	$0.00	$0.82	$0.00	$194.26	117.2606
Sub Total	$28,771.21	$1,071.23	$0.00	$0.00	$305.68	$0.00	$30,148.12	
Total	$28,771.21	$1,071.23	$0.00	$0.00	$305.68	$0.00	$30,148.12	

This example shows a yearly employee contribution of $5,731.28. In addition, the employer must make a matching contribution. Notice there is a vesting (when an employee has inalienable rights to money contributed by an employer to a pension fund or retirement plan after a certain number of years) of 100 percent. In this example, the employee has vested 100 percent in the matching contribution. The employer can require up to five years to vest in any match.

Just consider the comparison between an SEP and a 401(k) for a dentist with no eligible employees. The dentist makes $100,000 a year and takes the standard deduction.

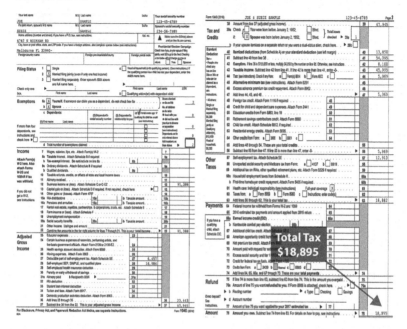

The dentist is able to put away 25 percent of their salary, and in this example, the salary is represented by the profit in the practice. The total tax bill in this scenario, with self-employment and income tax, is about $19,000. The dentist is able to put about $17,000 into an SEP.

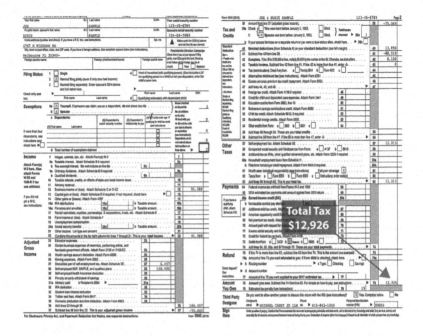

With a little more tax planning, here is the exact same professional with the exact same income:

By using a 401(k) with a profit-sharing option, we were able to set aside almost $40,000 more for retirement, plus we reduced the tax exposure by 25 percent. More money in your pocket and less money going to pay taxes is definitely a win-win situation.

If we went to the next step and offered a traditionally defined benefit plan (a pension), the amount of money that could be saved would be incredible. A defined benefit is different from a defined contribution in that the defined benefit sets the amount of income that a participant will receive during retirement. For example, some federal employees have a retirement benefit that pays 2 percent of their last three years' salary, per year of work.

This means that if the employee worked for forty years, their pension would be 80 percent of their salary. There are a few more rules involved with this calculation, but it serves as an example of how a defined benefit plan works.

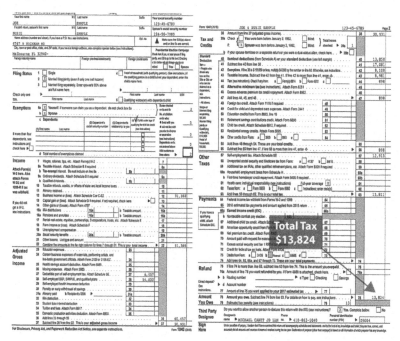

While the difference in tax savings is nominal, the amount contributed to the retirement accounts has gone from about $19,000 in an SEP to about $54,000 in a 401(k). Now, with a defined benefit plan, we are able to increase that contribution to $160,000. That is a substantial amount being saved toward retirement.

Additionally, the example provided here actually results in a loss on the tax return. Remember that the income was only $100,000, yet the dentist could save

$160,000. This means that the tax return will show a substantial loss. In this case, there is a loss being reported in the amount of $75,000. The dentist could then convert $75,000 from an existing IRA into a Roth and pay *zero* taxes.

In fact, it could be possible to get almost $60,000 into a Roth 401(k), almost another $160,000 going into a defined benefit, create a loss on the return, and have another $75,000 converted from a traditional IRA to a Roth.

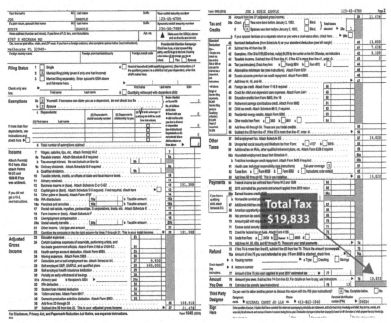

Let's look at another example. Let's assume the dentist's income is $300,000 instead of $100,000. Using a combination of tax-planning techniques, including a defined benefit, a defined contribution, and an employee welfare program, the dentist can put away almost

$225,000 toward retirement. With a $300,000 income, the total tax bill is less than $20,000.

What exactly is an "employee welfare benefit plan"? It is a very specific plan under Section 419, paragraph (e), of the Internal Revenue Code. The 419(e) plan allows an employee to set aside money to provide for retirement benefits covering such things as life insurance, health insurance, long-term care, and other medical expenses that arise after retirement. Imagine being able to use tax-deferred accounts to pay for your health care costs as you go through retirement *and* the ability to leave a legacy to your heirs through life insurance.

Plus, when planning is correctly done, the cash value of the life insurance policy can be extracted from the plan and can provide additional tax-free income during retirement.

Think about this for a minute. For a dentist (or any professional) who makes $300,000 in profit, the typical tax bill is almost $100,000. By taking time to sit down with a tax planner, not only did the dentist reduce their taxes by $80,000, but they also were able to save almost $225,000 for their retirement.

That is why tax planning matters, even for business owners.

At the end of the day, it doesn't matter how much you make; it is how much you keep. By taking the time to understand taxes and how they impact you today, as well as in retirement, you will give yourself the greatest opportunity to live your life and pay the least amount of taxes legally possible.

Your first step was reading this book. But that is only the beginning. Now you must use the knowledge you have gained to find the right advice giver. You need to find an advisor who is not only well versed in retirement planning but also in tax planning. You should ask them plenty of questions; we provided you with a list, which is a good starting point.

Don't let this information discourage you. It may take time to find the right advice since the field of those who understand both tax and investment planning is fairly narrow. It is further complicated by the number of CPAs and investment advisors who market themselves as tax planners but don't really go beyond the basics when it comes to getting you into the *zero* tax bracket.

That advisor should be able to show you their strategy to get you to the *zero* tax bracket. They should be able to tell you exactly how much should be in the taxable bucket. They should be able to calculate how much of your taxable bucket will be subject to ordinary tax rates and how much will be subject to capital gains tax rates. Remember, a properly structured asset allocation will result in your capital gains being in the *zero* percent tax bracket.

The advisor should be able to give you a step-by-step guide showing you exactly how much of your retirement accounts should be converted into tax-free Roth accounts, as well as how many years it will take in order to break even on the cost of conversion. Remember, you will pay taxes on the conversion, and the cost of those taxes is part of the calculation when it comes to a Roth conversion.

Finally, the advice should include whether you should use properly designed life insurance in your retirement plan. The benefits of using a properly designed policy are numerous: the ability to use the death benefit to cover the high costs associated with long-term care and the need for a nursing home; the ability to leave a legacy or to supplement the loss of pension income or Social Security upon your death; and (arguably the most important) the ability to create an additional bucket of tax-free income for you and your heirs.

Once you have found the right person, you can begin your journey toward a tax-free retirement. At that point, it won't matter if the government raises taxes in the future. When you are in the zero percent tax bracket, tax rates do not matter.

Paying zero taxes can't be a bad thing.

That is why tax planning matters.

Chapter 8

Bad Tax Investment Choices

As you have saved for retirement, you probably have received numerous offers of solicited and unsolicited advice. In many states, especially Florida, you can eat dinner five nights a week on the dime of some investment advisor or insurance agent hawking some iteration of "safe money." You can get more emails than you can ever review or read on why annuities are a great thing—or why Ken Fisher hates them and you should too!

It all starts with making the right choice of an advisor, right? A little history is in order here.

The Stock Market Crash of 1929 and the Resulting Securities Exchange Act of 1934

The Crash of 1929 is still considered the worst economic event in American history, maybe even in world history. Over the course of four days, the Dow lost 42 percent. When the crash started on October 24 of that year, some of the biggest banks, investment firms, and investors of that time stepped in to try to halt the slide. Morgan Bank (precursor to Morgan Stanley), Chase Bank, William Durant, Andrew Carnegie, the Rockefellers, and a host of other very powerful and wealthy families and businesses all attempted to halt the market from crashing. It helped, but only for one day. By the time November arrived, the market had resumed its slide and continued to slide until March 1933. Over a period of almost four years, the Dow lost a total of 89.2 percent.

The ensuing result was the election of Franklin Delano Roosevelt and the start of the New Deal. While there were many components of the New Deal, the law that still impacts investors today was passed in 1934. The passage of the Securities Exchange Act of 1934 was the response to the massive losses in the stock market and the impact that the Crash had on the average American investor. What specifically did the New Deal do?

Among other things, the New Deal created the Securities and Exchange Commission (SEC). The SEC is charged with overseeing securities: the buying and selling of stocks, bonds, mutual funds, variable annuities, and over-the-counter securities. It is also responsible for overseeing the conduct of financial professionals, including brokers, dealers, and investment advisors.

After the debacle of the 1929 Market Crash, the SEC, as part of its regulatory oversight, created a standard that all brokers must follow. These same rules established in 1934 are the same rules that today still govern the broker you have probably worked with in the past. The rule established that the broker is a middleman between you and the market, and they are there to help facilitate your purchase of investment products. Brokers must disclose certain things:

- They work for their company (called a broker-dealer or BD), not for you.

- Their duty of loyalty is to the firm for which they work (after all, the firm does provide their paychecks).

- They are not allowed to provide investment advice, but rather, they can ascertain whether a particular transaction is "suitable."

What does "suitable" mean?

According to the regulatory body that oversees brokerage firms and their employees (brokers, investment advisors, and registered representatives are among the many names they call themselves), Rule 2111 requires the following definitions of terms.

- **Reasonable-basis suitability** requires a broker to have a reasonable basis to believe, based on reasonable diligence, that the recommendation is suitable for at least some investors. Reasonable diligence must provide the firm or associated person with an understanding of the potential risks and rewards of the recommended security or strategy.

- **Customer-specific suitability** requires that a broker, based on a particular customer's investment profile, has a reasonable basis to believe that the recommendation is suitable for that customer. The broker must attempt to obtain and analyze a broad array of customer-specific factors to support this determination.

- **Quantitative suitability** requires a broker with actual or *de facto* control over a customer's account to have a reasonable basis for believing that a series of recommended transactions, even if suitable when viewed in isolation, is not excessive and unsuitable for the customer when taken together in light of the customer's investment profile.[16]

Notice that nowhere in that definition from the Financial Industry Regulatory Authority (FINRA) regulation does it mention anything about being *in the best interest of the client*. It actually says, "suitable for at least some clients," not "you" specifically, but "some clients." Nowhere does it mention avoiding conflicts of interest like selling proprietary mutual funds that carry higher-than-average management fees or that the broker earns higher commissions for selling specific products.

In addition, for the first time, the broker was required to actually take a test—a basic knowledge test. The name of the test is the *General Securities Representative Exam*. The name itself is important because it indicates that ultimately, the licensee is acting as a *representative* of the BD, not the client. Who do those registered representatives work for? You have probably seen their commercials on TV, or perhaps you have seen their name on the side of a tall building: Merrill Lynch, Wells Fargo, UBS, or Morgan Stanley—at least those are the last of the big wirehouses.[17] Along with these massive BDs, there are numerous small BDs out there that also follow the same suitability standards created in 1934.

---

16 https://www.finra.org/rules-guidance/key-topics/suitability

17 Wirehouse is an old term for a full-service broker-dealer whose employees work for the firm.

TWO PATHS TO BECOMING A FINANCIAL ADVISOR

	REGISTERED REPRESENTATIVE	INSURANCE AGENT
COMPANY	Broker-Dealer	Insurance Company
PRODUCTS/ SERVICES	Selling Investment Products	Selling Insurance Products
REQUIREMENTS	Series 6 or 7, and Series 63	State Life/Health Insurance License

It is important to understand this aspect of the New Deal. The New Deal does not require the broker to explain to you that the broker actually works for the brokerage firm; those types of advisors work for the firm. *They do not work for you. They work for somebody else.* They have a manager who tells the broker what they can and cannot do for the client. They have a manager who sets the quotas for the month, quarter, and year. The firm provides incentives for selling the most of something or for selling a certain dollar amount of some product. The firm actually tells them which investment choices they are allowed to offer the clients. As a matter of fact, you are not a client of the broker you are working with; rather, you are a client of the firm, and as soon as that broker leaves the firm, you will be assigned to the next twenty-four-year-old vice president in line for new clients.

Do you notice what else seems to be missing? Conflicts. There is no rule requiring the BD or the broker to disclose conflicts of interest. This is important to understand because most of these larger wirehouse firms also have an investment banking side to their practice. What is an investment bank? When a company wants to raise money by selling bonds (debt) or by issuing stock, they go through a middleman to facilitate the process. These wirehouses, or investment banks, are those middlemen.

For example, when Google wants to raise money in the capital markets or the stock market, they go to investment banks like Merrill Lynch, UBS, or Morgan Stanley. These wirehouses agree to handle and distribute the stocks to all the other firms (e.g., Fidelity, Schwab, Edward Jones, Ameriprise). These middlemen all agree to sell a certain amount of the stock within a targeted, specified price range. When the offering becomes available, would it be reasonable to assume that the advisors of all these firms recommend the stocks to their clients? Or at least their favorite clients? When an offering turns out like Google, we usually look at those results as a good thing.

But what about when they are recommending Enron? And how about when they are recommending mortgage-based credit default swaps? Remember those two debacles? Any worries about the firm getting paid large fees through solicitor agreements to push the sale of those stocks? If the firm received large fees to bring the offering to the table, do they have an incentive to push the sale of those positions over others?

It feels like there is an inherent conflict of interest. They get paid large sums to sell stocks to their clients, who pay them a fee to buy those very stocks. Is this perhaps a conflict?

An additional potential conflict of interest is that many of these larger wirehouse broker-dealers have their own proprietary funds. Anybody who has held accounts at Wells Fargo (WF) frequently sees Wells Fargo funds in their portfolios. This isn't to suggest that WF funds are bad funds—not at all. But it does beg the question: Did the Wells Fargo employee (your broker) recommend the WF fund because it was the best fund for you or because it pays them a better commission? Or perhaps because the manager requires a certain portion of assets to be allocated into WF proprietary funds? Does WF earn fees on managing the funds they offer to their clients?

Again, this is not to suggest that WF funds are inferior or that the broker is doing something "bad" to the client, but it does beg the question: Is the recommendation in the best interest of the client or just "suitable"?

As an investor trusting the advisor with your life savings, which do you want: a "suitable" investment recommendation or a recommendation in your best interest?

Think about it from this perspective: Imagine sitting down for dinner at a restaurant. The server gives you a menu of your options, and it looks like this:

For those of you who remember the movie *My Cousin Vinny*, this is the menu at the local restaurant. They were sitting down for breakfast and after reviewing the menu, they opted for "Breakfast."

Frequently, this is how a brokerage firm or wirehouse sells their products. They provide the broker with a menu of products that the *firm chooses* and then the broker sells those approved products.

What happens when you order the lunch, which advertises the price at $2.49? The server lets you know that it is a burger and fries. He asks how you want it cooked and whether you want lettuce, tomatoes, and pickles. Sounds good. When the plate comes out, it looks great. The only thing missing is ketchup for the fries, but that shows up immediately. When you are done, you ask for the check, and instead of seeing a bill for $2.49, it shows up as $21.00. Wait—how can that be?

Well, like working with a broker or wirehouse, frequently, the devil is in the details. Remember, they have a suitability standard, not necessarily a fiduciary standard. If they were a fiduciary, they would have told you that the lettuce, tomatoes, and pickles were all $2.49 each; that delivery to the table was another $2.49, and that the water you drank was also $2.49. Don't forget the ketchup, which is another $2.49. Don't forget the automatic tip included—the broker's version of a commission. All in all, you had a $21.00 lunch.

What does this actually have to do with taxes? It all revolves around those advisors who recommend mutual funds because they are told to sell them by their managers. Mutual funds, by their very design, typically are not tax efficient.

Remember Ken and Kathy from the very beginning of this book? Remember the tax implications of their owning mutual funds? We showed them the incredible tax liability they incurred *just because they own mutual funds*.

I. Last Year's Itemized Costs of Owning This Fund (WF Index Fund WFILX)

Itemized Fund Management Fees

1. Amount paid for fund administration	0.1960%
2. Amount paid in uncategorized fund management fees	0.282%
3. Total fund management fees you paid	0.48%
4. Amount paid for fund distribution	
5. Your share of the fund's transaction costs	
6. Taxes paid for holding the fund	7.02%
One-Year Total Cost of Ownership	**7.50%**

That is correct. For this S&P 500 Wells Fargo Mutual Fund, their estimated fees were over 7 percent.

When we looked at the mid-cap growth fund that their advisor had chosen for them, we discovered the following fees:

II. Last Year's Itemized Costs of Owning This Fund (WF Discovery Fund WFDAX)[5]

Itemized Fund Management Fees

1. Amount paid for fund administration	0.230%
2. Amount paid in fund advisory fees	1.182%
3. Amount paid in uncategorized fund management fees	
4. Total fund management fees you paid	1.41%
5. Amount paid for fund distribution	
6. Your share of the fund's transaction costs	0.38%
7. Taxes paid for holding the fund	3.39%
One-Year Total Cost of Ownership	**5.18%**

Notice line 7, which shows the taxes they paid for owning the fund. These are *huge* taxes. It isn't that the mutual fund generated those taxes just because they could. They were generated by the other investors in the mutual fund when they made the decision to sell their ownership interest.

Think about this for a minute. Remember back in 2008, when the market crashed? Many investors lost 30, 40, and even 50 percent of the value of their holdings. If you had that experience, you may also remember receiving a 1099B from the investment firm showing a capital gains distribution—a distribution that you then had to pay taxes on.

What? I lost 30 to 50 percent and I have to pay taxes on that loss? How is that possible?

Consider this example. Let's say that Apple stock was selling for a $1 a share in 1997 (just an example, not the actual cost). Let's also assume that Apple stock was worth $300 a share on January 1, 2008 (again, just an example). If by the time June came around and the market dropped—say, Apple went from $300 a share to $150 a share—isn't that a drop of 50 percent?

The problem is that when investors panic and want their money back, the manager of the mutual fund is forced to sell Apple stock for the current price of $150 a share. It is true that Apple was selling for $300, *but* the manager only paid $1 per share back in 1997. This means that even though the fund lost 50 percent for the year, the Apple stock actually had a gain on it from when it was purchased.

This is exactly how you wind up paying tax on a market loss. That doesn't sound like a smart strategy, does it? It's certainly not a strategy that an advisor looking out for *your* best interest would suggest—maybe one that has to answer to management and shareholders, but not one looking out for you.

For example, when suggesting an investment that represents the S&P 500 (remember, you can't invest directly into the S&P, but you can use a fund that tracks it), an advisor who has your best interest in mind might suggest something like Vanguard's VOO.

III. Last Year's Itemized Costs of Owning This Fund (VG Index VOO)

Itemized Fund Management Fees

1. Amount you paid for fund administration	0.020%
2. Amount you paid in fund advisory fees	0.003%
3. Amount you paid in uncategorized fund management fees	0.003%
4. Total fund management fees you paid	0.03%
5. Amount you paid for fund distribution	0.005%
6. Your share of the fund's transaction costs	
7. Taxes you paid for holding the fund	0.43%
One-Year Total Cost of Ownership	**0.46%**

Notice the difference in line 7? That is the difference between using mutual funds and using exchange-traded funds.

Tax planning matters.

Have you ever searched the internet for "variable annuity" or even just "annuity"? If you have, one of the most common thoughts when it comes to annuities is *I hate annuities and you should too*! It is a fairly well-known catch phrase, and if you have ever searched the internet by typing "annuities," all sorts of advertising comes up, explaining the horrors of using annuities.

I would suggest that these advertisements, sometimes disguised as useful information or advice, are actually just tactics used by various salesmen—biased, at that—to get you to invest your money in their flavor of the month.

If you really think about it, annuities are just a tool. Like any good tool, if used correctly, they can be very beneficial. Used incorrectly, they can be a disaster. A good friend of mine, John, is an electrician. For years, about once a month, John would gather up all his wrenches, pliers, and screwdrivers and take them up to Sears and replace them. When I asked him why he was replacing them so often, he explained that it is easier to use his wrench as a hammer when installing electric boxes than it was to carry around a hammer. He went on to say that rather than carrying around several testing wires because his pliers were insulated, he could test live circuits by just touching the tips to the black and white wires. True, it might blow the tips off the pliers, but it was easier than carrying around a big bucket of tools. Plus, evidently, Sears would guarantee Craftsman tools for life. For John, the promise of a lifetime supply of tools meant that he could take shortcuts.

I recently ran into John at BWI airport in Baltimore. He was working on a new wing of the airport. As we were catching up, I noticed he had a large cart full of tools and devices. I asked him, why all the tools? He explained that he recently changed his approach to using his tools. He had been testing, looking for a short in the wiring, and evidently, he found it! When he rubbed the tips of his pliers over the wires and he hit the live wires, he wasn't grounded properly (he was actually standing three steps up on a ladder) and he was blown off the ladder and against a wall about ten feet away.

He told me that he lay on the ground quivering for about fifteen minutes before he had the energy to stand up. His arm had been numb for weeks, he still had difficulty gripping tools with his right hand, and he had also been electrocuted almost a year earlier. John evidently decided that using the correct tool for the job made sense.

Using annuities is much like John and his approach to using tools. Using them correctly results in getting the job done right. Using them incorrectly can have disastrous results.

So why does Ken Fisher advertise that he hates annuities and you should too? The cynical answer is that he is a fee-based advisor and wants you to move your assets to his firm so he can charge you a fee to manage the assets rather than give them to some other firm that uses annuities—and gets paid a commission.

Having said that, there is some truth to what you read on the internet about annuities. Let's break down the main complaints that we have seen.

❶ They are very expensive to own.

Annuities can be very expensive to own depending on the type of annuity you purchase. Just like any investment vehicle, annuities come in all shapes and sizes. You certainly want to understand the fee schedule and know how those fees could impact your returns.

One type of annuity you can purchase is a fixed annuity. We'll talk more about them later, but basically, a fixed annuity smells and acts a lot like a certificate of deposit (CD). There's a *big* difference, though: the CD comes with FDIC (Federal Deposit Insurance Corporation) insurance protection, while a fixed annuity is only as strong as the issuing insurance company. More about this topic later.

Since we are discussing fees, how much does a fixed annuity typically cost to own, fee wise? Nothing. No fees. Zero. You can't get much cheaper than *zero*.

Conversely, you could also purchase a type of annuity called a variable annuity. Why variable? Because your returns vary—they are based upon the subaccounts you use inside the annuity (we'll talk more about them later as well). These types of annuities can be strapped with all sorts of fees: mortality and expense (M&E) fees, admin fees, subaccount fees (which also can have numerous types of fees inside of them), rider fees, possibly other fees for too many changes in the portfolio, or low balance fees, among others.

While these fees vary—I know, I see the humor—frequently the fee for the M&E is somewhere between 0.8 percent and 1.6 percent. The administrative fee is typically between $25 and $100. The subaccount fee (again, you'll understand these more as we refer back to them) can range from approximately 0.9 percent all the way up to 7 or 8 percent, and I have even seen higher fees. Then there are the rider fees, which can range from 0.25 percent up to 2 or 3 percent.

These are the fees that are usually the basis of complaints. After all, if you assume the stock market averages 6 to 8 percent returns over time, and you are being charged 3–5 percent or more in fees, how can you possibly expect to make money? You can understand why Mr. Fisher would tell you to hate annuities—at least variable annuities. You can see that there are fees associated with annuities, and certainly, the fees can be exorbitant, some as high as 5 percent or more. However, you must examine the annuity fees with those that come with using an investment advisor charging fees for advice and using investments like mutual funds, ETFs, and stocks, all of which can carry hefty fees as well.

Paying fees for services is nothing new. We pay fees for all sorts of things we find valuable: Netflix, cell phones, internet, gym and club memberships, and the list goes on. There is nothing necessarily wrong with paying a fee, as long as you know what you are paying and why—so ask. Ask the advisor you are working with; ask the insurance salesman you are working with. Ask the person or entity selling you the product or investment: *What are the fees?* Make sure you understand all the fees—not just the ones they want to tell you about, but also the "hidden" fees. We'll talk more about questions you should ask a financial advisor, planner, or insurance agent prior to making any investments or purchases.

❷ You can't make money in them because of the limits in the contract.

This complaint stems from two different issues: one, the fees greatly reduce the earnings on variable annuities; and two, the caps/spreads found in index annuities.

Let's look at the variable annuity (VA) first. If the goal is to make market returns along with market risk, then if you are going to use a VA (we'll discuss why people use VAs later), you will want to find the cheapest annuity (fee wise) with the best investment choices.

Did you know that Vanguard has an annuity you can use? According to their website, their total fees are less than 1 percent (M&E, investments, and admin) at investor.vanguard.com/home. Heck, that is cheaper than most mutual funds and maybe, just maybe, for the right reason, using a VA might not be so expensive after all.

T. Rowe Price has low-cost VAs. As a matter of fact, there are several very low-cost annuity companies offering variable annuities.

Clearly not all VAs are this inexpensive, and I suspect that most insurance agents and financial advisors earning commissions will not be recommending Vanguard VAs. Nevertheless, if you want growth and a VA is the right tool (again, we'll discuss later why it may be the right tool), you can find a very low-cost VA. Keep the fees down and you can make money when the market goes up.

As for index annuities, they are incredibly complex, and I am going to go out on a limb and suggest that most advisors/agents selling them really don't understand how the annuity can actually make money.

Without going into all the possible ways that index annuities "participate" in the stock market (more on that to come), equity index annuities (EIAs) won't see the same potential growth as something like an S&P 500 index fund.

EIAs frequently come with caps and/or spreads. Generically, the way these tools work is that if the EIA has a spread, the insurance company gets paid first. For example, if your EIA performance is based upon the performance of the S&P, and the EIA has a 3 percent spread, the first 3 percent that the EIA could possibly earn would go to the insurance company. If the EIA earned 6 percent on the underlying strategy and had a

3 percent spread, your account would only grow by the difference, or 3 percent.

The EIA could also have caps, which act as limits on how much you can earn. For example, if the EIA has a 6 percent cap on the underlying strategy and that strategy earned 17 percent, you would only be credited the 6 percent.

If you are going to use an EIA for growth purposes, you certainly need to understand how the caps/spreads are going to impact your ability to make money. The advisor/agent who presents an EIA to you should be able to articulate how you can actually make money. You certainly want them to go through the nuances of how the caps and/or spreads are going to impact your potential growth.

You could ask yourself, "If it is so hard to make money in them, why would I purchase one?" We'll address that question in a later chapter.

❸ They have huge surrender charges.

That could be true. Many annuities come with time constraints, and if you cash out—that is, take all your money out within a certain period of time—you could be charged surrender fees. Sometimes these fees are draconian; I have seen fees as low as 1 percent, but also as high as 24 percent. Most fall into the 4–12 percent range, but still, imagine having to pay 10 percent in surrender fees just to get your money?

Most of these annuities that carry surrender charges have a sliding scale. For example, if you take 100 percent of your money in the first year, your surrender charge may cause you to lose 12 percent of the value of the distribution; in the second year, the charge would be 11 percent; the third year, 10 percent; and so on. Obviously, each insurance company has its own surrender schedule and, depending on the type of annuity you purchase, that surrender schedule could be as short as one to four years or as long as ten to twenty years. This is why it is so important to understand how you are going to access your money.

Just like investing in the stock market, most annuities are considered long-term vehicles, so you should never make any investment into an annuity or the stock market if you will need access to 100 percent of the funds in the near future.

If you choose to use an annuity, make sure you understand the liquidity features and how you are going to access your money should you need it. Also, remember that there are numerous annuities out there that carry no surrender charges at all. There are also annuities that have a "return of premium" feature that allows you to access 100 percent of your principal within a specified period of time. You may lose part or all of your gains, but you can walk away with your principal.

❹ They pay commissions.

Again, this is a mostly true statement. Certainly, the majority of annuities being used by advisors carry some sort of commission. The question is whether the advisor/agent recommended the annuity because it was the best tool for you or because it paid a hefty commission.

How hefty? I have seen annuity products that pay as little as 1 percent, but I have also seen commissions as high as 14–15 percent. In years past, there were annuities that would pay upward of 20 percent in commissions. As of this writing, most annuities that pay commissions pay between 3 and 7 percent.

That question should be answered, right? Does the person recommending the annuity really think it is good for me? Or does this person just need to meet a sales quota or make a mortgage payment?

We all know that if we are working with somebody who is going to provide advice, they are going to get paid for giving that advice. Nobody works for free (and that includes those free dinners and lunches to which you get invited). It is reasonable for them to get paid—they have the knowledge, and you are seeking their assistance.

So should you hate annuities because of the commission? Let's explore that a little more. Let's assume for a minute that we agree that purchasing an annuity is a long-term purchase. Let's assume that you are going to take a "buy-and-hold" approach and not use *all* of the money for the next ten years. And finally, let's assume that you are investing $100,000.

If you use a fee-based advisor who charges you 1 percent over a period of ten years, you will have paid the advisor $10,000 in fees over the course of that ten years. That fee, by the way, comes out of your money. So all things being equal, assuming a 0 percent return for the ten-year holding, your account balance would be $90,000 (your $100,000 initial investment less the $10,000 in advisor fees).

Using the same facts with the same return of zero, the annuity would have $100,000 at the end of the ten-year holding period because the agent's commission comes out of the insurance company's pocket, not your investment. Your investment is not reduced in any given year for the commission(s) paid to the advisor.

To be fair, we didn't include any underlying investment fees, and such fees would clearly have an impact on your balance over that ten-year time period. We wanted to use an apples-to-apples comparison to show how much those commissions actually cost you, the investor.

It is very fair to ask how the advisor gets paid. If an advisor recommends an annuity, it should be to accomplish a very specific goal. Never purchase an annuity (or make any investment) that isn't based upon a goal just because you can—the goal should always dictate the investment. Purchase an annuity because it fits your needs. By making sure it fits your needs, you can then judge whether the recommendation was to earn a commission or because it was the right choice for you.

❺ They are inherently difficult to understand.

Did you just read the previous pages? These things are inherently confusing, so it's no wonder that regulators are watchful over these vehicles.

There are a lot of moving parts in an annuity:

- caps
- spreads
- volatility
- fees
- surrender charges
- liquidity
- tax consequences
  - safety

Trying to piece them together along with all of the other factors that come with deciding whether an annuity is appropriate can be very overwhelming.

An annuity is just another tool. Don't hate them. Make sure you understand annuities and certainly ask questions.

- An annuity can come in many shapes and sizes. Make sure you understand which type you are buying.

- An annuity can come with huge fees. Make sure you understand how much you will be paying for *all* the fees.

- An annuity usually isn't very liquid. Make sure you know when and how you will have access to your money.

- Always put in the least amount necessary to accomplish the goal that the annuity is designed to address.

- And finally, make sure you understand how your annuity is actually going to make money for you.

Open-heart surgery is inherently difficult to understand. That doesn't mean people shouldn't have the surgery. They should have the surgery when it is the right thing for them—just like using an annuity.

So, again, what does all this have to do with taxes? While we don't object to using an annuity when it is the right tool, we do have concerns about the tax implications of using an annuity.

An annuity works in a very similar way with taxes as an IRA, 401(k), or any other type of retirement account. You don't pay tax on the growth or interest until such time as you actually use the money. This means that the annuity has tax-deferred growth opportunities. I get to invest in or buy an annuity, and I don't have to pay any taxes on the growth until I actually need to use the money. You can take money from your investment accounts or bank accounts—those very mutual funds you paid tax on when the market dropped—and put them into an annuity, and you won't pay one penny in taxes until you actually withdraw money from it. You will pay no tax at all until you actually need it.

That sounds wonderful.

The real reason Mr. Fisher should hate annuities, and specifically nonqualified annuities, is that by using *after-tax* dollars (qualified money uses pre-tax dollars), you have changed the tax nature of all future growth. Remember, if you have money in a brokerage account at Charles Schwab, Fidelity, or even one of those wirehouses or broker-dealers, your gains on your investments are typically taxed at capital gains rates, not ordinary income rates.

For example, if you need to take $50,000 out of your brokerage account, assuming it was all gains for simplicity's sake, your tax rate would be between 0 and 15 percent. As a matter of fact, with the current capital gains rates in place, your tax rate would be *zero*. You could actually get all of your $50,000 out without paying one cent in taxes.

However, what if you take that same $50,000 of profit out of your annuity? You would be taxed at your ordinary tax rate, somewhere between 12 and 22 percent.

Sound confusing? This is why most firms do not allow their advisors to provide any sort of tax guidance or advice.

Remember what we said at the beginning of the book? How can anybody provide investment advice and not understand the tax implications of that very advice?

Zero percent or 12–22 percent? Tax planning matters.

Chapter 9

Conclusion

In previous sections, we outlined many details of tax strategy examples and why taxes matter. One effective way to prove these examples and truly comprehend the realm of possibilities is to use the three basic tax buckets. Those three basic tax buckets are:

① **Taxable**

② **Tax Deferred**

③ **Tax Free**

Now that you have read this book, which bucket do you think your money should be in?

Put It in the Tax Buckets!

There is a mathematically ideal amount of money to have in each bucket. Your goal should be to have three to six months of expenses set aside in a safe and secure place for emergencies. These funds will be in a **taxable bucket**. You may also consider having additional resources set aside in a taxable bucket, but you will want to make sure that the bucket is subject to capital gains taxes, not ordinary tax rates. This is the Warren Buffet rule: Never pay a higher tax rate than a clerical worker!

Your **tax-deferred bucket** should hold no more money than would cause your Social Security to be taxable when taking your required minimum distributions. This means that your RMDs should be less than the standard deduction on your tax form, which in 2021 was about $12,550 for singles and $25,100 for taxpayers who were married filing jointly.

If the goal is to keep your RMDs under the standard deduction, then an ideal amount in these accounts should be somewhere between $150,000 and $300,000. Of course, you will need to calculate how the RMD will impact your Social Security. Ultimately you want no more in your retirement accounts so that when you add your RMDs into your income, it does not cause your Social Security to be taxable.

The balance of your money should be in the **tax-free bucket**: Roth IRAs, Roth 401(k)s, and properly designed cash-value life insurance.

By following this approach of tax efficiency, you will not be in a place where you worry that the government may raise taxes in the future. If you have designed your retirement income plan properly and have funded your money buckets correctly, you will retire with tax-free income.

They say that there are two things in life you can't avoid: death and taxes. While these are words of wisdom and have been uttered down through the generations, this book has given you the necessary information so you may be able to at least avoid most of the taxes.

It is well known that here in the United States of America, tax avoidance is legal, but tax evasion is not. Tax evasion opens up the possibility of criminal charges for the offenders. You have very likely heard of the famous case that supports the legal description of tax avoidance philosophy.

We now add those oft-quoted lines from the most recognizable tax judgment for *all* American taxpayers handed down by Judge Learned Hand:

> *Anyone may arrange his affairs so that his taxes shall be as low as possible; he is not bound to choose that pattern which best pays the treasury. There is not even a patriotic duty to increase one's taxes. Over and over again the Courts have said*

that there is nothing sinister in so arranging af-
fairs as to keep taxes as low as possible. Everyone
does it, rich and poor alike and all do right, for
nobody owes any public duty to pay more than
the law demands.[18]

Judge Learned Hand

Judge, U. S. Court of Appeals

In the simplest terms, there is nothing wrong with structuring your assets, your income, and your estate to reduce or eliminate the need to pay income taxes. Reading this book is the first step toward having a completely tax-free retirement.

Overall, making these kinds of investments in your future takes commitment, expertise, and support. As you have learned in the pages of this book, tax planning matters! This overall change takes time and planning. However, with the information in this book, you now have the tools and knowledge in order to make smart money choices as well as smart tax choices.

What you do next is yours to do.

---

18 As quoted in:
Gregory v. Helvering 69 F.2d 809, 810 (2d Cir. 1934),
aff'd, 293 US 465, 55 S.Ct. 266, 79 L.Ed. 596 (1935)

About the Authors

Charles Bartman

CEO, president, and founder, Senior Financial Center

 CHARLES BARTMAN is a recognized financial professional, gifted writer, and established speaker at public and company educational events. Charles co-authored the book *Safer Income for Life* and has published articles in *Forbes*, *Money Magazine*, *CNN Money*, and numerous other media outlets. He has also appeared on Jane Pauley's CBS *Sunday Morning* show as a host of his "Sunday Morning Money Report," been featured on the radio with his "Monday Morning Report," and hosted his radio show, *Safer Income for Life*.

Charles's dedication and commitment have enabled him to guide his clients to achieve their retirement goals. He focuses on utilizing downside market protection for retirement income planning, reducing excessive fees, maximizing Social Security to collect more money, and employing tax-forward planning to reduce your taxes to get you as close to ZERO as possible. Advisors will talk about the proper allocation of clients' assets, but many don't discuss the proper allocation of investible assets to reduce taxes by hundreds of thousands of dollars.

Charles believes that it's not how much you make; it's how much you keep.

David Bartman

Vice president, Senior Financial Center

DAVID BARTMAN is recognized as one of the nation's leading experts on retirement strategies. His passion is assisting his clients in or near retirement to understand their money and protect their assets. He gives his clients the information they need to make truly informed decisions. David understands the unique challenges his clients face in all aspects of their lives and is specifically trained to assist them from the accumulation stage of their assets to the preservation stage to the distribution stage, avoiding excessive and unnecessary taxes.

He understands that with longer life expectancies, people are concerned that they will outlive their money. David has counseled hundreds of clients in retirement around the country for many years. David has preserved millions of dollars in retirement assets by assisting his clients in flexible investment strategies. These principles are what he has based his business on. David's clients rely on his advice to sustain their lifestyle and build and preserve their wealth. He listens to each client he meets with to determine what's important to them. People feel comfortable working with him because of the level of integrity he demonstrates when dealing with such delicate issues as one's personal finances. David works tirelessly to achieve their goals. He understands that his clients always come first, and his commitment is to work with them to develop lifelong relationships based on their needs and values.

Michael Canet, JD, LLM

Owner, Prostatis Financial

MICHAEL "MIKE" CANET helps people create, grow, protect, preserve, and distribute wealth in the most tax-efficient manner. Whether the client is an average American just entering into retirement or a complex multigenerational family looking into protecting wealth, Michael helps clients maximize their assets and plan for the future using advanced tax planning. He uses retirement and estate planning techniques to carefully allocate clients' assets so that they can retire with added confidence, income, and tax-deferred wealth protection. He reminds his clients that it doesn't matter how much they make but, rather, how much they keep at the end of the day that really counts.

Michael is an active industry contributor to television, radio, and print. His numerous publications can be found in 100 different periodicals and journals across the country, including *WSJ*, *Forbes*, and *USA Today*. He has contributed to a variety of periodicals, journals, and books, including *Successonomics* by Steve Forbes and the Amazon #1 Best Seller *Surviving the Perfect Storm: How to Create a Financial Plan That Will Withstand Any Crisis*. Michael has been seen on every major network as a financial commentator and has hosted a nationally syndicated television and radio show, *The Savvy Investor*. You can find his talks and interviews on a variety of radio and major network shows in the Baltimore/Washington area, Central Florida, as well as the Space Coast of Florida, including FOX, NBC, CBS, and ABC.

In addition to working at his own firm, Michael is also a sought-after mentor and business practice coach, speaking and working with hundreds of financial advisors every year to help them in their own firms. In this capacity, Michael serves as CEO advisor for almost two dozen advisors around the country and represents over $1 billion in assets.

Michael is quick to share his personal history and how his upbringing influenced his approach to business and philanthropy. He grew up living in children's shelters and the foster care system, experiencing various highs and dysfunctional lows. As Michael moved within the social welfare system, he recognized the many incredible people who provided him with the stability and encouragement he needed to thrive. Today, Michael commits to giving back as much as he can by helping those less fortunate. These causes include the Maryland Volunteer Lawyer Service (where Michael was named Volunteer of the Year) and a position on the UB President Advisory Board, where he helps guide the university in its efforts to reach and educate a diversified student body. His firm has helped to raise and donate over $150,000 to causes like Make-A-Wish, the Ronald McDonald House, Ray's Summer Days, the Maryland Food Bank, Generosity Global, the Animal Welfare Society, the Harold & Carole Pump Foundation for Cancer Prevention, back-to-school supply programs, and a host of others. Michael continues to put his family and loved ones front and center for himself, his firm, and his clients. He has been married for thirty-nine years and has two incredible sons. Michael takes great pride in the stability he has been able to provide to his own family, stating that he wanted to make sure that they never experienced what he went through. A devoted family man and husband, he counts his blessings while at home, where he enjoys entertaining, cooking, and collecting wine. Michael splits his time between Ellicott City, Maryland, and Melbourne, Florida, and is an enthusiastic world traveler, exploring food and culture on five (and counting!) continents with his favorite travel partner, his wife.

For more information on Michael, go to ProstasisFinancial.com.

Glossary

Investment Term Definitions

The following terms and definitions are meant to be helpful in understanding various investment and financial terms. The definitions provided are general in nature and are not intended to be definitive explanations of the various financial terms contained herein. For a comprehensive and exhaustive explanation and understanding of these terms, please consider using a dictionary or the internet.

401(k) plan:

An employer-sponsored, IRS-qualified plan that permits employees to make pre-tax contributions from their wages to a profit-sharing plan, a target benefit plan, or a stock bonus plan. The great news is that contributions and earnings grow tax deferred until withdrawn.

403(b) plan:

A retirement plan for employees of nonprofit organizations, public schools, and churches where employees can contribute a portion of their wages to a mutual fund or annuity. As with a 401(k) plan, the great news here is that contributions and earnings grow tax deferred until withdrawn.

Adjusted gross income (AGI):

This is the amount of income on which a person computes deductions that are based on, or limited by, a percentage of his or her income to figure out federal taxable income. The AGI is determined by subtracting from gross income any deductible business expenses and other allowable adjustments (some traditional IRA annual contributions, SEP and Keogh annual contributions, and alimony payments).

Administrator:

A person appointed by a probate court to handle the estate of a person who died intestate (without a will). This person has the same duties as an executor.

Advisor:

See definitions for *Financial advisor* and *Investment advisor*.

Annuity:

A contract that provides for a series of payments to be made or received at regular intervals. An annuity may be immediate, starting as soon as the premium has been paid, or it may be deferred, starting at a designated later date. Annuities are commonly used to fund retirement. (See also *fixed index annuity* or *variable annuity*.)

Assets:

Property and tangible resources, such as cash and investments. Examples include stocks, bonds, real estate, bank accounts, and jewelry.

Asset allocation:

An investment strategy for the purpose of enhancing total return and/or reducing risk by diversifying assets among different types of stocks, bonds, and money market investments.

Beneficiary:

An individual, institution, trustee, or estate that receives, or may become eligible to receive, benefits under a will, insurance policy, retirement plan, annuity, trust, or other contract.

Bond:

Basically an IOU or promissory note of a corporation, usually issued in multiples of $1,000. A bond is evidence of a debt on which the issuing company usually promises to pay the bondholders a specified amount of interest for a specified length of time, and to repay the loan on the expiration date. In every case, a bond represents debt. Its holder is a creditor of the corporation and not a part owner, as is the case with a shareholder.

Brokerage:

A security transaction executed through a brokerage firm or broker/dealer in stocks, bonds, mutual funds, options, or other investment securities. This term is often mistakenly used for the brokerage firm itself, but it actually refers to the transaction.

Certified public accountant (CPA):

An individual who has received state certification to practice accounting.

Commission:

A broker's basic fee for purchasing or selling securities or property as a registered representative.

Death benefit:

A payment made to a beneficiary from an annuity or life insurance policy when the policyholder dies. Also called *face amount* or *face value*.

Deductible:

Relating to health insurance, a predetermined amount that the insured person pays for medical treatment before the health insurance coverage kicks in.

Defined benefit plan:

A company retirement plan, such as a defined benefit pension plan, in which a retired employee receives a specific benefit based on salary history and years of service, and in which the employer bears the investment risk. Contributions may be made by the employee, the employer, or both.

Defined contribution plan:

A company retirement plan, such as profit sharing, money purchase pension, 401(k), or 403(b), in which each participant has an individual account within the plan with benefits based solely upon amounts contributed and the past performance of that account. The participant bears the investment risk.

Diversification:

Spreading investments among different companies in different fields. Another type of diversification is offered by the securities of many individual companies because of the wide range of their activities.

Dividend:

A payment designated by the board of directors to be distributed pro rata among the shares outstanding. Preferred shares generally pay a fixed dividend, while common shares pay a dividend that varies with the earnings of the company and the amount of cash on hand. Dividends may be omitted if business is poor or the directors withhold earnings to invest in plant and equipment. Sometimes a company will pay a dividend out of past earnings even if it is not currently operating at a profit.

Equity:

The ownership interest of common and preferred stock-holders in a company. Also refers to the excess of the value of securities over the debit balance in a margin account. Also refers to the value of a property that remains after all liens and other charges against the property are paid. A property owner's equity generally consists of his or her monetary interest in property in excess of the mortgage indebtedness. In the case of a long-term mortgage, the owner's equity builds up quite gradually during the first several years because the bulk of each monthly payment is applied not to the principal amount of the loan, but to the interest.

Exchange-traded funds:

An investment vehicle traded on stock exchanges, much like stocks. An ETF holds assets such as stocks or bonds and trades at approximately the same price as the net asset value of its underlying assets over the course of the trading day. Most ETFs track an index, such as the S&P 500 or MSCI EAFE. ETFs may be attractive as investments because of their low costs, tax efficiency, and stock-like features.

Financial advisor:

A person employed to provide advice on subjects related to investing and personal financial decisions.

Financial plan:

A plan with stated goals and objectives pertaining to the current and long-term investment needs of the individual.

Financial planning:

Creating a plan with stated goals and objectives pertaining to the current and long-term investment needs of the individual.

FINRA:

FINRA is an independent regulatory organization empowered by the federal government to ensure that America's investors are protected. (See also *NASD*.)

Fixed index annuity:

An annuity contract issued by an insurance company that earns interest based on gains in a market index and/or a fixed rate of return. The interest rate is guaranteed to never be less than zero with no loss of principal from market declines. Payments can be lump sum or flexible with income deferred or immediate.

Health insurance:

Insurance that provides protection against financial losses resulting from illness, injury, and disability. In general, any insurance program covering medical expenses and/or income lost owing to illness or accidental injury.

Heir:

An individual who will receive assets upon the death of another individual.

Income taxes:

Taxes on income, both earned (salaries, wages, tips, commissions) and unearned (interest from savings accounts, stock dividends). All individuals and businesses are subject to income taxes.

Individual retirement account (IRA):

A tax-advantaged personal retirement account that allows a person to invest each year. A contribution may be tax deductible depending on your adjusted gross income, whether you're married, and whether your employer offers a retirement plan at work. A rollover IRA accepts eligible employer-sponsored retirement plan assets.

Interest:

An amount charged by a lender to a borrower for the use of money. Interest rates are normally expressed in terms of an annual basis.

Internal Revenue Service (IRS):

The federal agency responsible for administering and enforcing the Treasury Department's revenue laws through the assessment and collection of taxes, determination of pension plan qualification, and related activities.

Investment:

A current commitment of money for a period of time to obtain future payments or wealth to compensate the investor for the time the funds were committed for the inflation that may affect them and for the uncertainty of repayment.

Investment advisor:

A person employed to render advice or analysis about securities/ and investments for compensation registered with the SEC under the Investment Advisers Act of 1940 or their respective state. Does not include attorneys and accountants who give advice as a part of their professional practice.

Investment company:

A company that owns a diversified portfolio of securities that are professionally chosen and managed on the basis of certain investment criteria. The most common type of investment company is the mutual fund.

Investor:

An individual whose principal concerns in the purchase of a security are regular dividend income and/or capital appreciation without unnecessary risk.

Liabilities:

A broadly defined term implying legal or financial responsibilities to others.

Life insurance:

Insurance coverage against death of a person to be paid to a beneficiary when the insured dies. (Types include *term insurance, whole life insurance, universal life insurance, variable life insurance,* or *survivorship life insurance.*)

Liquid:

A description of the condition in which an individual has adequate cash and near-cash assets to meet current debt.

Long-term care:

Physical, mental, and social assistance provided to people who are unable to provide for themselves as a result of disability or a prolonged illness. Care ranges from providing personal care at home, such as bathing and dressing, to skilled nursing services in a nursing home.

Medicaid:

A program, funded by the federal and state governments, that pays medical costs for the poor. If your financial assets and monthly income are below certain allowed levels, Medicaid will pay nursing home and some home care costs if you are disabled.

Medicare:

A federal program that pays for certain health care expenses for people aged sixty-five or older.

Morningstar:

A leading provider of mutual fund, stock, and variable-insurance investment information. As an independent company, Morningstar does not own, operate, or hold any interest in mutual funds, stocks, or insurance products.

Mutual fund:

An open-end investment company that continuously offers new shares to the public in addition to redeeming shares on demand as required by law.

NASD:

Refers to the National Association of Securities Dealers, Inc., an association of brokers and dealers in the over-the-counter securities business. The association has the power to expel members who have been declared guilty of unethical practices. The NASD is dedicated, among other objectives, "to adopt, administer, and enforce rules of fair practice and rules, to prevent fraudulent and manipulative acts and practices and, in general, to promote just and equitable principles of trade for the protection of investors." The NASD has been replaced by FINRA.

Net worth:

The amount by which a person's total assets exceeds their total liabilities.

Online:

A technology service provided over computers that are networked together. Usually refers to the internet. Allows for interaction between people via computer.

Planning:

The act of contemplating objectives, desires, and variables to accomplish an objective. Examples are current investments, rates of returns, and retirement income desired for an individual's financial plan.

Portfolio:

A group of securities held by an investor. They might include stocks, bonds, preferred stock, or cash.

Principal:

As it relates to power of attorney, a principal is the person who is no longer able to make decisions to the point where the attorney-of-fact is granted the power to make those decisions.

Retirement income:

The amount of income needed, on an annual basis, to live once the investor has retired. Can be pre-tax (the amount needed for spending, plus the taxes due on that amount) or after-tax (the amount needed for spending to meet their lifestyle, excluding taxes).

Retirement plan:

A person's unique plan for meeting his or her retirement obligations, or an employer-sponsored tax-advantaged program to accumulate assets for the retirement of the plan's participants.

Return:

The dividends or interest paid by a company expressed as a percentage of the current price. A stock with a current market value of $20 a share that has paid $1 in dividends in the preceding 12 months is said to return 5 percent ($1/$20). The current return on a bond is figured the same way. Another term for yield.

Rider:

An amendment to an insurance policy that modifies the policy by expanding or restricting its benefits or excluding certain conditions from coverage.

Risk:

Uncertainty that an asset will earn its expected rate of return, generally measured using the standard deviation.

Risk tolerance:

The measure of an investor's ability to accept risk. Investors are often categorized as risk-indifferent, risk-averse, or risk-seeking.

Roth IRA:

A personal retirement savings vehicle created by the Taxpayer Relief Act of 1997, available for certain investors beginning in 1998. A Roth IRA allows certain investors to make nondeductible contributions annually, provided that certain requirements are met, and offers (after owning the Roth IRA for five years) tax-free and penalty-free withdrawals for important specified financial needs as qualified distributions. Distributions after age fifty-nine and a half are tax free, provided you have had the Roth IRA for five years before you withdraw funds.

Savings account:

A bank account established for the purpose of putting aside money for future spending goals. Savings accounts normally earn a competitive rate of interest and are insured by the Federal Deposit Insurance Corporation (FDIC).

Share:

A certificate representing one unit of ownership in a corporation, mutual fund, or limited partnership.

Social Security:

The government-sponsored program that is designed to provide basic pensions and disability income for US citizens.

Standard deduction:

The amount a taxpayer who does not itemize his or her federal tax deductions can deduct in determining taxable income.

Stock:

Ownership shares of a corporation that provides the lender with a claim on a company's earnings and assets. Stock may be issued in different forms, including common and preferred. Holders of common stock are the last to be paid from any profits from the company but are likely to profit most from the company's growth. Owners of preferred stock are paid a fixed dividend before owners of common stock, but the amount of the dividend doesn't usually grow if the company grows.

Tax deductible:

An item or expense subtracted from adjusted gross income to reduce the amount of income subject to tax. Examples include mortgage interest, state and local taxes, unreimbursed business expenses, and charitable contributions.

Tax deferral:

Paying taxes in the future for income earned in the current year, such as through an IRA, 401(k), SEP IRA, or Keogh Plan.

Tax-deferred retirement plans:

A retirement plan in which you get to postpone current income taxes on pre-tax money invested or any earnings in an account until you withdraw it from the plan. Such a plan may allow you to set aside part of your pay for retirement. Tax-deferred accounts include traditional and rollover IRAs and 401(k)s.

Trusts:

A legal arrangement in which an individual (the trustor) gives fiduciary control of property to a person or institution (the trustee) for the benefit of beneficiaries.

Variable annuity:

A contract created by insurance companies that allows you to invest your money within an investment portfolio (called subaccounts) similar to mutual funds that could include stocks, bonds, and so forth. Unlike other annuities, a variable annuity will not guarantee any equities within the subaccounts.

Vested:

The rights of an individual to receive benefits from employment, such as pension, sick leave, and vacation. Pension benefits are vested when the employee has worked a specified number of years. The person may then leave the employer for another job and still collect the accumulated amount at retirement.

Volatility:

The extent to which the value of an investment changes. Often used as a description of risk and measured in standard deviations.

www.ExpertPress.net